AF739109

Human Nature and the Discipline of Economics

Religion, Politics, and Society in the New Millennium

Series Editors: Michael Novak, American Enterprise Institute, and Brian C. Anderson, Manhattan Institute

For nearly five centuries, it was widely believed that moral questions could be resolved through reason. The Enlightenment once gave us answers to these perennial questions, but the answers no longer seem adequate. It has become apparent that reason alone is not enough to answer the questions that define and shape our existence. Many now believe that we have come to the edge of the Enlightenment and are stepping forth into a new era, one that may be the most religious we have experienced in five hundred years. This series of books explores this new historical condition, publishing important works of scholarship in various disciplines that help us to understand the trends in thought and belief we have come from and to define the ones toward which we are heading.

Political Memoirs, by Aurel Kolani, edited by Francesca Murphy

Challenging the Modern World: Karol Wojtyla/John Paul II and the Development of Catholic Social Teaching, by Samuel Gregg

The Scepter Shall Not Depart from Judah: Perspectives on the Persistence of the Political in Judaism, by Alan L. Mittleman

In the World, But Not of the World: Christian Social Teaching at the End of the Twentieth Century, by Andrew L. Fitz-Gibbon

The Surprising Pope: Understanding the Thought of John Paul II, by Maciej Zieba, O.P.

A Free Society Reader: Principles for the New Millennium, edited by Michael Novak, William Brailsford, and Cornelis Heesters

Beyond Self-Interest: A Personalist Approach to Human Action, by Gregory R. Beabout, et al.

Human Nature and the Discipline of Economics: Personalist Anthropology and Economic Methodology, by Patricia Donohue-White, et al.

The Free Person and The Free Economy: A Personalist View of Market Economics, by Anthony J. Santelli Jr., et al.

Meaningless: The Solutions of Nietzsche, Freud, and Rorty, by Michael A. Casey

FOUNDATIONS OF ECONOMIC PERSONALISM

Series Editor: Stephen J. Grabill, Research Fellow, Center for Economic Personalism

Foundations of Economic Personalism is the series title for three jointly authored monographs, each analyzing a significant dimension of the Center for Economic Personalism's unique synthesis of Christian personalism and free-market economic theory. In the aftermath of the momentous geopolitical changes of the late 1980s, a small group of Christian social ethicists began to dialogue with free-market economists over the morality of market activity. This interdisciplinary exchange eventually led to a new research program within Christian social ethics under the rubric of *economic personalism*. Economic personalists strive to integrate economic theory, history, and methodology with Christian personalism's emphasis on human dignity, humane social structures, and social justice.

Beyond Self-Interest:
A Personalist Approach to Human Action
by Gregory R. Beabout, Ricardo F. Crespo, Stephen J. Grabill, Kim Paffenroth, and Kyle Swan

Human Nature and the Discipline of Economics:
Personalist Anthropology and Economic Methodology
by Patricia Donohue-White, Stephen J. Grabill, Christopher Westley, and Gloria Zúñiga

The Free Person and The Free Economy:
A Personalist View of Market Economics
by Anthony J. Santelli Jr., Jeffrey Sikkenga, Rev. Robert A. Sirico, Steven Yates, and Gloria Zúñiga

Human Nature and the Discipline of Economics

Personalist Anthropology and Economic Methodology

BY

PATRICIA DONOHUE-WHITE
STEPHEN J. GRABILL
CHRISTOPHER WESTLEY
GLORIA ZÚÑIGA

CENTER FOR ECONOMIC PERSONALISM
FOUNDATIONS OF ECONOMIC PERSONALISM SERIES
EDITED BY STEPHEN J. GRABILL

A division of
ROWMAN & LITTLEFIELD PUBLISHERS, INC.
Lanham • Boulder • New York • Toronto • Plymouth, UK

LEXINGTON BOOKS

A division of Rowman & Littlefield Publishers, Inc.
A wholly owned subsidiary of The Rowman & Littlefield Publishing Group, Inc.
4501 Forbes Boulevard, Suite 200
Lanham, MD 20706

12 Hid's Copse Road
Cumnor Hill, Oxford OX2 9JJ, England

Copyright © 2002 by Lexington Books

All rights reserved. No part of this publication may be reproduced, stored in a retrieval system, or transmitted in any form or by any means, electronic, mechanical, photocopying, recording, or otherwise, without the prior permission of the publisher.

British Library Cataloguing in Publication Information Available

Library of Congress Cataloging-in-Publication Data

Human nature and the discipline of economics : personalist anthropology and economic methodology / by Patricia Donohue-White . . . [et al.].
p. cm.—(Religion, politics, and society in the new millennium)
Includes bibliographical references and index.
ISBN 0-7391-0184-6 (alk. paper)—ISBN 0-7391-0185-4 (pbk. : alk. paper)
1. Human beings. 2. Man (Theology) 3. Economics—Philosophy. I. Donohue-White, Patricia. II. Series.

BD450 .H859 2001
306.3—dc21

2001029265

CONTENTS

PREFACE

In recent decades, we have witnessed a flourishing of interdisciplinary studies throughout the academy. Subjects once considered, at best, peripheral to particular intellectual disciplines if not generally irrelevant, are now reflected on by scholars who have spent much of their working life focused on reasonably narrow areas of intellectual endeavor.

In general terms, this development should be welcomed. It reflects a significant effort on the part of some scholars to redress the excessive specialization that characterizes much of the academy. There are, however, significant risks involved in this process. Scholars are just as susceptible as everyone else to the temptation to write and speak about issues and subjects of which they have little knowledge and with disregard for the established evidence that has been accumulated throughout the ages.

It was, therefore, more than a risk for the Acton Institute's Center for Economic Personalism to bring together theologians, economists, and philosophers to converse about, and to study collaboratively, the subject of this second of the three volumes in the *Foundations of Economic Personalism* series. The profound differences that underlie the methodological underpinnings of the disciplines of theology, philosophy, and economics are not incidental. They often reflect views of the nature of the human person that are at deep variance with one another. There is clearly no room for compromise between, for example, the utilitarian view of human beings advocated by Jeremy Bentham and, to a lesser extent, John Stuart Mill, as little more than pleasure-maximizing machines, and the Christian understanding of man as a spiritual-material creature who is called to a transcendent destiny but also capable of actions that are intrinsically evil.

How, then, one might ask, is it possible to begin a meaningful conversation between disciplines such as economics and moral theology? The answer is surely that contained in the methodological proposition articulated by the phenomenologist, Edmund Husserl: *zurück zum Gegenstand* (back to the object). In this case, the "object" of study to which we are called to return is the human person. By identifying the key elements of this creature that makes him or her different from the animals, theologians, economists, and philosophers can establish common ground for engaging in both an adequate moral analysis of the economic realities that surround us, as well as reflect on the adequacy of the variety of economic theories and propositions that play such a profound role in shaping the public square and human culture.

If such a conversation is to be meaningful, then it cannot pretend that difficulties do not exist, or that there are no points of incompatibility between economics and Christian ethics. One of the strengths of this second volume is that these problems are acknowledged. But it is precisely because of the recognition of these obstacles that the authors of this volume are able to delineate the often-overlooked points of agreement between theology, moral philosophy, and economics as intellectual disciplines. The authors do not, of course, claim to have resolved all of the relevant problems. They do, however, establish the parameters for a clearer and more disciplined discussion of this complex but important subject.

Samuel Gregg
Director, Center for Economic Personalism
Acton Institute for the Study of Religion and Liberty
Grand Rapids, Michigan

INTRODUCTION

Personalism in the History of Political Economy

Though most thoroughly developed in the twentieth century, personalism as an intellectual current has not been foreign to economic thought. Within the history of economic thought, forms of personalism have actually exerted a strong influence. Any economic analysis that presents descriptive models of human behavior has recognized, if only implicitly, the importance of basing its system on a correct understanding of the human person. While this aspect of social science has received more attention in the last twenty years, this does not mean that personalism's influence is a modern phenomenon. Actually, modern personalist thinkers have constructed their systems based on intellectual precedents from earlier eras, which they reorganized and synthesized into what is called personalism today.

While personalism's influence can be found in any social science, the personalist influence in economic thought stands out. Notions of the centrality of the human person were essential to the economic writings of Thomas Aquinas and the Scholastic thinkers who followed him. This thread was expanded upon, largely by the Physiocratic writers battling the reigning mercantile influences of mid-eighteenth-century Europe. While the Physiocrats are also associated with some of the greatest absurdities in the history of economic thought, their system was quite revolutionary. Many of its positive aspects were incorporated by Adam Smith into his magnum opus, *The Wealth of Nations*. J. B. Say, writing from France in the generation that followed Smith, instilled personalist thought into his system; this contrasted with the English classical economists who built on

Smith but who became so wedded to the cost-of-production theory of value that the uniqueness of the human element was de-emphasized. However, personalist elements in economic thought continued to develop on the Continent, where Say's influence was as great as Smith's in the English-speaking world. Carl Menger's use of personalist principles is prominent in his explanation of the valuation process. Today, modern Austrian economists' focus on the individual is linked to the personalist writings in economics from the past.

What follows is a summary of personalist writings gleaned from the history of economic thought. By presenting personalist influences in economics from the past, we intend to show that such an effort is not foreign to economics and is, in fact, perfectly congruent with it. Indeed, a full understanding of economic thought would be incomplete without an understanding of human agency and human action.

Scholasticism

The goal of scholasticism, in the tradition forged by Thomas Aquinas, was to develop a body of logic and philosophic thought built on a Catholic understanding of the world, including an emphasis on natural-law ethics. This body of thought sought to address a wide number of theological, scientific, and social problems. This ambitious intellectual project provided an opportunity for Scholastic theorists to explore areas now classified under economics, including property, trade, money, interest, prices, and wealth creation. The Scholastics agreed generally that the way to understand economics was by reflecting on the preferences, purposes, outlook, and intentions of economic actors themselves and observing how they impress themselves on a physical world of limited resources. This approach differs from that of the Greeks, who began their analysis from the "things" that the economy produced. The Scholastics offered a foundation for economics that began with an analysis of human action and human nature. From its foundation in human cognition, Thomist economic thought became refined through the centuries, culminating in the sixteenth-century School of Salamanca in Spain, a primary center of learning and commerce.

The history of Scholastic economics begins with the Franciscan San Bernardino of Siena (1380-1444), who raised the status of businessmen to a higher moral plateau than had previous theorists. The transitional figure from Bernardino to the Late Scholastics is Thomas de Vio, Cardinal Cajetan (1468-1534), who spelled out what was then the state-of-the-art in monetary theory. From Cardinal Cajetan's Italy, the torch passed to Salamanca and to the Dominican founder of Salamancan economics, Francisco de Vitoria (1485-1546), who was one of the early founders and intellectual patrons of the School of Salamanca.

Under the guidance of Vitoria the university grew to offer more than seventy chairs in academic subjects. Like many other influential teachers, much of Vitoria's thought comes to us through the class notes of his students. His main innovation came with his comments on price determination.[1] Instead of having cost of production determine market value, Vitoria, while stating that cost could well be considered, returned to the old, nearly forgotten laissez-faire Roman Law tradition of free individual bargaining, to provide the just price. Precedent existed, Vitoria maintained, for prices to be settled by the exchanging parties themselves.[2]

Dominican student Domingo de Soto (1494-1560), for example, insisted that "the price of goods is not determined by their nature but by the measure in which they serve the needs of mankind."[3] He also regarded it as a "natural right" that a man can "donate or transfer the things he legally owns in any way he wants."[4]

Martin de Azpilcueta Navarrus (1493-1586), a student of de Soto, would further Salamancan economic ideas. Both de Soto and Navarrus denounced as fallacious the notion of John Duns Scotus (1266-1308) that the just price is the cost of production plus a reasonable profit. Instead they argued that prices were expressions of the common estimations of value as understood in terms of supply and demand.[5] Navarrus even developed a clear and logical refutation of all price controls in the form of either ceilings or floors, and an equally clear theory that the value of money is inversely related to the amount available in the economy.[6]

Luis Saravia de la Calle (c.1544) denied any role to cost in the determination of price; instead the market price—the just price—is determined by the forces of supply and demand, which, in turn, are the results of the cumulative estimations of consumers on the market.[7] He went on to argue that the price of a thing will change in response to its abundance and scarcity.[8]

The greatest student of Navarrus was Diego de Covarrubias y Leiva (1512-1577), considered the best jurist in Spain since Vitoria. The emperor made him chancellor of the Castile, and he eventually became bishop of Segovia. In his *Variarum* (1554) Leiva sets value theory back on the right track: The value of goods, according to him, depends not on matters intrinsic to the good or its production but on the estimations of consumers. Thus, writes Leiva, "the value of an article depends on the estimations of men, even if that estimate be foolish. Wheat is more expensive in the Indies than in Spain because men esteem it more highly, though the nature of the Wheat is the same in both places."[9]

Luis de Molina (1535-1601) was one of the earliest Jesuits to devote attention to economic concerns. Though devoted to the Salamancan School and its achievement, Molina taught in Portugal at the University of Coimbra. Following upon the work of Leiva, Molina refined aspects of a subjective value theory further. By way of criticizing Duns Scotus and his followers, Molina made it clear that production cost, although a factor in the determination of exchange value, was not its source or cause:

> In the first place, it should be observed that a price is considered just or unjust not because of the nature of the things themselves—this would lead us to value them according to their nobility or perfection—but due to their ability to serve human utility. Because this is the way in which they are appreciated by men, they therefore command a price in the market and in exchanges. Moreover, this is the end for which God gave things to man, even though they belonged to everybody at the moment of their creation. What we have just described explains why rats, which according to their nature, are nobler than wheat, are not esteemed or appreciated by men. The reason is that they are of no utility whatsoever. This also explains why a house can be justly sold at a higher price than a horse and even a slave, even though the horse and the slave, are by nature, much nobler than the house.[10]

The use of a particular good is not fixed between people or with the passage of time. It changes according to individual valuations and availability. Molina's theory also explains peculiar aspects of luxury goods. For example, why would a pearl, which can only be used to decorate, be more expensive than grain, wine, meat, or horses? As Molina explained, valuation is done by individuals, and we can conclude that the just price for a pearl depends on the fact that some men wanted to grant it value as an object of decoration.

A similar paradox that befuddled the classical economists was the diamond–water paradox. Why should water, which is more useful, be lower in price than diamonds? Following Scholastic logic, it is due to individual evaluations and their interplay with scarcity. Molina was careful to point out that utility was not a property of the goods themselves or identical with any of their inherent qualities, but rather the estimations of importance attached to these goods by consumers.

In all, the School of Salamanca represents a major episode in the history of economic thought. It forged the beginnings of a tradition of economic theory that began to take persons and their valuations seriously. Joseph Schumpeter, in his *History of Economic Analysis*, observes that "it is within their systems of moral theology and law that economics gained definite if not separate existence, and it is they who come nearer than does any other group to having been the 'founders' of scientific economics."[11] By placing the locus of analysis on the individual human mind and rejecting utopian fantasies of transforming the natural law to accommodate another view, the Late Scholastics created an economics that is both theocentric and anthropocentric. Economics, like all worldly philosophy, must center on God, because the world is God's creation and the individual is created in God's image; likewise, humankind's creative intentions and purpose, to an extent, reflect the creative intentions of God Himself.

The Physiocrats

The Physiocrats were a group of political economists based in France during the middle of the eighteenth century. Considered to be the first scientific school of economics,[12] the Physiocrats enjoyed enormous influence throughout Europe and the United States until they were eclipsed by Adam Smith and the classical school of economics, which began with the publication of *The Wealth of Nations* in 1776. As is often the case with new intellectual currents, Physiocratic thought developed in response to an established order that was losing credibility in a rapidly changing world. The mercantile system had characterized economic life in Europe since the Middle Ages. This system was based on the belief that extreme governmental involvement in economic affairs was necessary in order to maintain specie flows into the country. As a result, it protected monopolies, and huge public and private bureaucracies ruled the day. When the middle classes started to form for the first time in Europe, the inefficiencies of the dominant economic system became obvious to larger and more powerful segments of the population. The Physiocrats countered the dominant mercantilist system by developing their own economic approach. By presenting a consistent logic of economics, the Physiocrats formed the basis from which future schools of thought would develop.

The Physiocrats were imperfect in large part because of their identification with *Tableau Economique*, or Economic Table. This was an input–output table showing the movement of wealth through a country. The Physiocrats considered the *Tableau* to be among the greatest accomplishments of humankind, and they aligned their legitimacy as a school closely with that model. They lost credibility when the *Tableau* was discredited; and today most economists will associate the *Tableau* with the Physiocrats.[13] This unfortunate development is not undeserved given the extent to which Physiocratic thinkers praised the *Tableau* and its creator, Francois Quesnay. However, this identification causes many to underestimate the contributions to economic thought made by the Physiocrats, many of which were supplanted by Adam Smith. Unfortunately, by embracing Smith's system, future economists discarded many personalist applications to economics that were still in their formative stages.

The recognition of a priori truths is an important element of personalist thought. This concept had a strong influence in economic thought long before the Physiocrats, although there had never been as great a defense of a priori truths until their school became a viable intellectual force. The Physiocrats recognized the existence of such truths in their writings on the natural law, which led to their defense of laissez-faire. They recognized the importance of these truths that governed individual persons for economic analysis, and, in the process, incorporated a primary tenet of personalism into economic thought.

The Physiocrats believed in the rule of the natural law over the actions of individuals in the formation of society.[14] They knew that the natural law was difficult for the human mind to define and to understand, but concern for the natural law represented a concern for the human person. Only those individuals who are governed by the natural law, or by as few man-made laws as possible, would live a fully human life, because they were shaped by the order of nature to the greatest possible extent. The Physiocrats thought that stronger adherence to natural laws would also result in a sounder economic system. While such talk was revolutionary during the height of the mercantile era, today their identification of the natural order with an agricultural economic order is considered to be their greatest blunder. Yet, it should not be forgotten that the Physiocrats insisted that economic theory should be shaped around an accurate idea of the human person. Economic action was based on the needs of the individual, not those of certain classes or societies. They thought that "through the proper employment of men, in conformity with the particular advantages at the disposal [of a given country], that the nation can cause its revenue to expand."[15] The proper employment would encompass those activities that were in accord with the natural law.

The Contribution of J. B. Say

Adam Smith soon followed the Physiocrats and quickly eclipsed them. His system also focused on both the individual and on the nature and creation of wealth. As such, there is not much of interest to personalism in his writing that had not been established already by the Physiocrats, from whom he borrowed much of his conceptual apparatus. The examination of the individual as the center of economic organization took a backseat to an emphasis on issues such as wealth, population, and wages; at least on the part of those political economists who built upon Smith's system. This marked a setback for the development of economic personalism. However, the inroad of personalist concepts into economics continued on the Continent. This development is especially notable in the writing of Jean-Baptiste Say.

J. B. Say (1767-1832) was a French businessman who developed an interest in political economy into one of the most famous books in the history of economic thought. His *Traité d' Économie Politique* extended much of what was useful in Smith's system, reinserting into political economy notions about the primacy of the individual as the center of attention. This strongly influenced analyses of value and wealth and eliminated a long-run steady state toward which the economy was inevitably headed. The focus on the individual marked Say's parting with the tradition of Smith. For Smith, it was not necessary to make assumptions about human nature in order to maintain the logical framework of his schema. However, Say's schema was founded upon a realistic assumption of the human person—or, at least, as realistic as possible given the theoretical and cultural understanding of his time.

In 1794, Say became the leader of a group of philosophers called the *Décade*. These men were devoted to the study of all forms of human action as the basis of political economy. Say's work represents an effort to understand the individual human person, and from that understanding, to construct the case for a sound political economy. His disagreements with Smith can be interpreted as disagreements over the role of the person in society. While Smith and his followers extolled the individual, their efforts were aimed at facilitating the creation of wealth. For Say, this goal was of secondary importance to the formation of a logical and consistent political economy. When the overriding goal of an economic school is the creation of wealth, the purpose of economics can be overlooked. Wealth creation is an important area of interest to political economists, which was also certainly the case in Say's time. However, to make this study the sole object of a school of thought leads to the neglect of other important aspects of political economy. As detailed later, Say's stress on the individual prompted him to reemphasize the role of the entrepreneur in economic theory, an element that was completely ignored by Smith and those who followed in that tradition.

Like those writing in the personalist tradition, Say rejected the necessity of employing mathematical and statistical techniques in analysis of economic phenomena. He thought that they trivialized economic theory, while ignoring important human relationships that are not open to measurement. In this way, Say articulated the proto-personalist concern for the effects of technology on the human person, because such mathematical and statistical conventions represent nothing more than changes in methods of examination. He was not opposed to analytic technology per se but was concerned about its effect on human beings. Policies that would follow from such models would effect damage on the economy because, since their conclusions were not based on the real world, their effects would have even worse consequences in the real world where they would be implemented.

Furthermore, Say would have supported the personalist understanding of a priori truths that comprise the human person, and as a Catholic, he would have been comfortable with the statement that human beings have a soul as the first a priori truth. The economic conclusions that derive from that statement are completely different than those that follow from a mathematical or statistical schema. His economics was rooted in natural-law theory, which set Continental economics apart from that which developed in the English tradition of Smith, where utilitarian thought developed into the neoclassical economic paradigm that still dominates today. All of the implications of his system had to be founded on natural law. He differentiated his reasoning from that of the Physiocrats, since his natural-law leanings did not cause him to embrace agriculture as the basis of legitimate economic formation.

Say's discussion of the origin of value demonstrates his commitment to the human person as the central focus of analysis. Value results from the moral and physical nature of man, the climate in which he lives, and from the manner and legislation of his country.[16] Ideas such as the cost of production or use value, which make sense outside of a personalist schema, are not even considered. To Say, subjective human desire creates value.

Say's greatest contribution to economic thought is his discussion of the entrepreneur. Since we take the entrepreneur for granted today, Say's explanation of the importance of this economic actor sounds trivial. The fact that entrepreneurs were ignored in Smith's system illustrates the differences between the classical school and that which developed on the Continent. The idea of an individual risking his or her own wealth in order to provide for the needs and wants of others recognizes the central importance of the individual. The economic system of an entrepreneur is not like a machine that chugs on, regardless of human interaction. Instead, human interaction fuels the system, and the entrepreneur instigates each instance of this action. While the Smithian writers of Say's day focused on a long-run equilibrium toward which economies inexorably grew, Say's discussion of the entrepreneur correctly recognized the ability of individuals to adapt and to affect the economic system.

Conclusion

Though our historical survey of the personalist aspects of economics could continue, this chapter serves merely to show that various points of contact already exist between economics and theology, particularly in terms of personalist ideas and theological anthropology.

Our task in the remaining chapters, however, is to sharpen the interdisciplinary conversation that is the central aim of economic personalism. The next several sections include presentations by our team of theologians and economists. Each presentation emphasizes the contextual and methodological issues of their respective fields of study. The theologians explain the history and meaning of personalism, its development in response to philosophical and theological trends, and its possible application to economics. Above all, they concentrate on articulating the anthropological vision of personalism. The economists, on the other hand, perform a similar task, only they explain the methodological parameters of their discipline and—to a limited degree—explore its historical development. Throughout this process, the economists describe the underlying anthropological assumptions of their discipline.

What we hope to gain, in addition to greater mutual understanding, is a precise comprehension of the significance of anthropology to moral theology and economics. It is our belief that a correct vision of the human person is the essential starting point in the generation of scholarship for a humane economy. The twentieth century has witnessed the shipwreck of socialist economics and social engineering. The fundamental problem with socialism was not its impracticality, inefficiency, or poor management of resources. Rather, the flaw of socialism, and the reason it failed to produce a humane society, was because it failed to comprehend critical dimensions of human nature.

The ensuing discussion of methodology, anthropology, and economic personalism seeks to provide an alternative vision for economics from both the usual reductionist tendencies of neoclassical economists and socialist collectivism. This conversation is worth having for its own sake, even if our results may prove tentative or the disciplinary fissures become more pronounced. Our conviction is that the more accurate and realistic the anthropology, the better the chances that economics can contribute to the development of a humane social order.

Notes

1. Murray N. Rothbard, *Economic Thought before Adam Smith: An Austrian Perspective on the History of Economic Thought*, vol. 1 (Hanks, U.K.: Edward Elgar, 1995), 60, 80, 101, 103.
2. Rothbard, *Economic Thought*, 102-3.
3. Rothbard, *Economic Thought*, 103.
4. Alejandro A. Chafuen, *Christians for Freedom: Late-Scholastic Economics* (San Francisco: Ignatius Press, 1986), 60.
5. Rothbard, *Economic Thought*, 105.
6. Chafuen, *Christians for Freedom*, 106.
7. Murray N. Rothbard, "New Light on the Prehistory of Austrian Economics," in *The Foundations of Modern Austrian Economics*, ed. E. G. Dolan (Mission, Kans.: Sheed and Ward, 1976), 54-55.
8. Luis Saravia de la Calle, "Instruccion de Mercadres (1544)," in *The School of Salamanca: Readings in Spanish Monetary Theory, 1544-1605*, ed. and trans. Marjorie Grice-Hutchinson (Oxford, U.K.: Clarendon Press, 1952), 79-82.
9. Saravia, "Instruccion de Mercadres," 86.
10. Luis de Molina, *La Teoria del Justo Precio* (Madrid: Ed. Nacional, 1981), 167-68.
11. Joseph A. Schumpeter, *History of Economic Analysis* (New York: Oxford University Press, 1954), 97.
12. John F. Bell, *A History of Economic Thought* (New York: Ronald Press, 1967), 102.
13. Cf. Schumpeter, *History of Economic Analysis*, 239-43.
14. In fact, the term *physiocracy* means rule of nature. It was coined by

Pierre Samuel du Pont de Nemours in 1768.

15. Roland L. Meek, *The Economics of Physiocracy: Essays and Translations* (London: George Allen & Unwin, 1962), 89.

16. Schumpeter, *History of Economic Analysis*, 615-17.

1

Theological Anthropology and Personalism

What Is Theological Anthropology?

Theological anthropology comprises the study of the human person and the human condition in history. Christian anthropology approaches the human person first and foremost as a theological being, that is, as a being essentially and fundamentally in relation to God. Other humanistic disciplines that ignore this aspect fail to present as rich and accurate a picture of what is certainly distinctive of the human person. And though it may draw upon the many other humanistic disciplines, theological anthropology attempts to transcend purely human experience and, through both general and special revelation, grasp a vision of the human person that is more and other than merely human.

Theological anthropology concentrates on the fundamental doctrines of the Christian faith relative to the origin, condition, and destiny of the human person: the original creation of the human being in the *imago Dei* (the image of God), the corruption of human nature through sin, the redemption of the human person through the life, death, and resurrection of Jesus Christ, and the final fulfillment and completion of that redemption in eternal life with God. It thus approaches the human being in terms of three distinct, though interrelated, states or conditions: the condition of original created goodness, our historical condition as corrupted by sin and open to redemption, and the eschatological state, that is, final union with God in eternal life. Though it focuses particularly on the actual, historical condition of the human person, theological anthropology would not be complete if it did not consider this actual state in relation to both the origin and destiny of the human person.

The understanding of the person that emerges from theological reflection on the human condition is complex, dynamic, and incomplete. It encompasses revelation and human experience, nature and grace, faith and reason. It focuses on the action of God relative to the human person (creation, incarnation, and redemption) and the human response to God. It conceives of the human situation as one of dynamic tension, a tension rooted in our historicity and freedom.

As historical beings we are always incomplete and open to the future. We develop ourselves in time and within particular historical and cultural contexts. However, we are also simultaneously destined for a life with God beyond history. As finite, sinful beings, we are structured by tendencies toward immanence, sin, vice, corruption, and death. Yet, as free persons loved by God, we are called to transcendence, goodness, communion with others, and eternal life with God. Theological anthropology recognizes the human person as an agent in history and sees the drama of human life as unfolding through human action. Nonetheless, it insists that God is the Lord of history who acts on our behalf by continually sustaining us with his grace and life.

Theological anthropology is unavoidably doctrinal in its fundamental concepts and categories, for example, original sin, incarnation, grace, and redemption. Within the context of the present work, we draw principles and concepts from Christian anthropology that we think can be articulated in nontheological language and understood by practitioners in nontheological disciplines. In order to attain this goal, however, it is necessary that theological anthropology be permitted to proceed according to its own methodology and terminology.

Dimensions of the Human Person and the Human Condition

Because theological anthropology recognizes the dynamic, complex, and incomplete character of the human person, one cannot derive from it simple and fixed models of human nature. Nonetheless, it is possible to identify certain dimensions of the person that are constitutive of and foundational to the human condition.

The Dignity of the Human Person As Created by God

In recounting the story of creation, Genesis 1:26 teaches that the human person is made in the "image and likeness of God." This passage has remained the starting point for theological anthropology throughout the history of Jewish and Christian thought.[1] The human person understood as created in the image of God establishes our unique value and dignity. We are creatures willed into being by the Author of the universe. The concept of the imago Dei encompasses various dimensions of the human person. Principal among these are the human capacities of reason and will, our essentially communal or social character, and the capacity for relationship with God.

The imago Dei refers to the fact that human beings are spiritual subjects capable of reasoning, understanding, responding, and acting. Though humans are located in the natural realm as finite living beings, as persons, they are capable of transcending the dynamism immanent to biological life by maintaining a relationship to the world and other persons in acts of understanding, creativity, and self-determination.

Though this emphasis on the spiritual character of the person has at times been construed to suggest a dualism of soul and body with an accompanying reductive notion of the body, modern orthodox Christianity consistently maintains that the human person as the imago Dei is an integrated unity of spiritual and vital dimensions, a unity of body and soul.[2] Orthodox Christian belief excludes any form of biological reductionism, while affirming that the body is a dignity-maintaining dimension of the person.

The imago Dei also refers to the social or communal dimension of the person. People were created to be in relation with others. The rationale behind being in relation with others is not rooted merely in our dependence upon others, that is, our lack of self-sufficiency. It expresses, rather, the deepest orientation of the human soul: to join with others in common activities for common purposes, to be bound to others in relations of co-responsibility and self-giving love. At its best, personal communion is to be patterned after the union of persons within the Trinity.

Finally, the imago Dei refers to the human capacity for being in relation to God. The human person is not only created and loved by God, but also capable of knowing God, participating in his life, and reciprocating the love with which God first loved us. This meaning of the imago refers to the human capacity for transcendence in its deepest and truest sense and reveals the ultimate origin and destiny of the human person.

To summarize, the imago Dei is the idea that humans are radically concrete, subjective, unrepeatable beings, who are loved by God and ordered to personal communion with one another. As such, the term *person* encompasses both the individuality and the essentially relational (or communal) character of the human being. It emphasizes the unique value and dignity that persons possess by virtue of their humanity without retreating to an atomistic individualism. It also designates the essentially communal character of the person without falling prey to collectivism. Finally, it affirms the significance of human freedom for personal life without severing that freedom from values, truth, and love.

The Corruption of Sin

The actual human situation is one where human nature is marred and corrupted by sin, a situation in which the original image has been obscured and effaced. These effects must be considered on two primary levels. On the first and deepest level, sin refers to a fundamental rupture between humanity and God, a rupture for which humanity alone is responsible. Sinful people turn away from God, thus causing their participation in God's life to be spoiled. In Emil Brunner's words, "in the last resort, [sin] is the denial of God and self-deification: It is getting rid of the Lord God and the proclamation of self-sovereignty."[3]

As a consequence of this rupture, the nature of the person is deeply affected. This brings us to the second level. Our fundamental separation from God does not simply mean a loss of relationship. It radically affects the structure and character of our being so that through sin we become inclined toward immanence, vice, corruption, and death. The second level refers to the consequences of sin for human nature and the human condition.

Interpretations of the consequences of sin upon human nature have generated significant divisions among Protestants and Catholics. On the one side is the Augustinian and Reformed position, which claims that human nature, particularly the will, is so deeply corrupted by sin that humans do not choose God in matters pertaining to salvation. Steeped in sin, the will is naturally inclined toward selfishness, vice, and inflated notions of self-sufficiency. Thus, according to this view, grace is needed to restore humanity's relation to God and to reorder the natural capacities of the human person, particularly reason and the will.

Augustine's position took form in his controversy with Pelagius. According to Pelagius, the capacity to know and to do the good, though impaired by sin in the individual and society, remains intrinsic to human nature in such a way that grace is not strictly required for persons (1) to transform their nature and (2) to begin the work of being reconciled to God. Against the first proposition, Augustine argued that while the human will remains free in that it is not subject to external compulsion, the capacity to choose the good for its own sake cannot be recovered apart from grace. For Augustine the capacity to choose remains inherent to human nature, but without grace this capacity would be governed by pride and self-serving desire.[4] Only the grace of God can heal and transform the will and thus free the person to do the good for its own sake. Against the second proposition, Augustine insisted that only grace could restore the broken relationship between humanity and God. This position was developed further by the Protestant Reformers of the sixteenth century.

On the other side is the position of Justin, Irenaeus, and many Late Scholastics (e.g., Gabriel Biel), according to which the human person, though affected by sin, retains essentially intact the capacities of reason and will. Irenaeus argued that all persons, because of their creation by the benevolent and just God, possess a free will that holds them accountable for their actions. In his reading of the creation narrative in the first chapter of Genesis, Irenaeus distinguished between humanity as created in God's image and humanity as created in God's likeness.[5] The creation of humans in God's image refers to the essentially good nature of the human person, whereas the creation of humans in God's likeness refers first to the perfect man Jesus Christ and then to humans who are conformed to Christ. Likeness-to-God means participating in God's Spirit and as such is not inherent to human nature nor is it achievable through human effort. Being remade in the likeness of God is a gratuitous gift bestowed by God that can be retained or revoked through the use of human freedom.

For Irenaeus, sin does not destroy the goodness of human nature. Even after the Fall, persons are capable of knowing the truth, willing the good, and seeking God. Without this capacity, Irenaeus argued, we could not be held responsible for our actions. However, because of sin the gift of God's Spirit has been lost to humanity as a whole. As sinners, we cannot reconcile ourselves to God through our own action. Thus for Irenaeus, we retain not only our negative freedom, that is, freedom from coercion, but also the positive capacity to choose good over evil. Irenaeus argued that while this capacity may be corrupted through the misuse of our freedom, it has not been utterly effaced.[6]

The Late Scholastics built on Irenaeus' concept with their distinction between nature and the supernatural. The latter term refers to the super-added righteousness given by God to the human person through grace, the former to the natural capacities of freedom and will. While sin results in the loss of supernatural grace, it does not distort nature in such a way that the capacities of reason and will become naturally inclined to ignorance and vice.

These two extremes constitute the limits of Protestant and Catholic orthodoxy and indicate the Scylla and Charybdis of, on the one hand, a Pelagianism that denies the reality of sin and the necessity of grace, and on the other, a determinism that denies human freedom and responsibility. A large middle ground exists between these positions, each of which expresses the paradoxical character of the human condition differently: People are simultaneously selfish, vicious, and evil, and yet good, virtuous, and kind.

Redeemed by Grace in Jesus Christ

The Christian faith affirms that God freely chose to become human in the person of Jesus Christ in order to reconcile humanity with himself. Jesus Christ, as God and man, is the full self-revelation of God and the revelation of true humanity. For this reason, the study of the person and work of Christ (or Christology) becomes a starting point of Christian anthropology, since Jesus Christ, by assuming human nature, reveals to us the true and perfect human form and, through his suffering and death, reconciles us with God.

This Christ-centered approach to anthropology (understanding the nature and condition of the human being in terms of the God–man Jesus Christ) characterizes the theology of some of the most influential twentieth-century theologians, particularly Karl Barth and Henri de Lubac. We briefly examine the anthropology of these thinkers in conjunction with a number of other influential contemporary theologians, concentrating primarily on the understanding of human freedom and action that emerge from their work.

Survey of Theological Anthropology

Protestant Theology

Karl Barth, Emil Brunner, and Reinhold Niebuhr developed their theologies in critical reaction to the liberal German theology of the nineteenth and early twentieth centuries (e.g., Friedrich Schleiermacher, Albrecht Ritschl, Adolph von Harnack, Albert Schweitzer, and Wilhelm Herrmann). They each attempted to return Protestant theology to its roots in the theology of the Reformers and to reassert the primacy of God's special revelation in Jesus Christ.

Liberal Protestantism of this era believed in the perfectibility of human nature, immersed itself in contemporary culture, and was critical of orthodox Christianity. This self-criticism consisted of subjecting the Christian faith to severe philosophical and historical criticism. While neoorthodox theologians sympathized with some of the impulses of liberalism (both Barth and Niebuhr were converts from liberalism), they also identified tendencies within liberalism that led to serious distortions in understanding the Gospel and the human situation. Contrary to liberalism's tendency to reduce the Christian life to ethics and Christ to a moral ideal, neoorthodox theologians reasserted the primacy of faith in the historicity of the person of Jesus Christ. Neoorthodox theologians emphasized the transcendence of God and the priority of God's actions relative to humanity (creation, incarnation, and redemption) over and against the liberal stress upon religion as an inner experience of self-discovery. Particularly in response to the world wars, neoorthodox theologians rejected liberalism's optimism concerning human perfectibility, emphasizing instead human brokenness and crisis.[7]

Emil Brunner: The Contradiction Between Humanity As It Is and As It Was Intended to Be

Emil Brunner's *Man in Revolt* is one of the more significant works of contemporary theological anthropology. Brunner was not only critical of liberal Protestantism, but also of the tendencies within orthodoxy to reduce faith to abstract doctrinal truths and to neglect the existential situation of the human person.

Brunner insisted that religious belief arises from and reveals the deepest dimensions of the human situation. Since the human situation is characterized by paradox and contradiction, Brunner argued, theology must be dialectical. That is, it must draw out the contradictory character of the human condition. At the same time, it must affirm the primacy of the God who meets us in our crisis. Drawing on the thought of Søren Kierkegaard, Ernst Ebner, and Martin Buber, Brunner also understood his theology to be a biblical personalism. In contrast to the God of the philosophers who is abstractly conceived, the God of the Bible is a person, the absolute subject. The person of God cannot be confined to human conceptuality. He is a person who intrudes into our thoughts and experience, who makes himself known and calls us to respond to him. The relation between God and the individual is a deeply personal one in which the human being is called and addressed as a person, that is, as an individual subject capable of personal response.[8]

Brunner's theological anthropology starts from the fundamental human experience of the self as a riddle, a paradox, or a question. We are the only beings who not only question the world around us but also engage in self-criticism. We are fundamentally dissatisfied with our situation and ourselves; we are not at home in the world or with ourselves. We are divided beings, experiencing constant tension between that which we are and that which we desire to be.[9] Historically, we cannot avoid seeing the contradiction between human creativity, achievements, and refinement on the one hand, and human misery on the other.[10]

Though various explanations for this contradiction have been advanced, Brunner argues that it is Christianity that reveals the truest and deepest source, since the human being is inescapably theological: "that is, his ground, his goal, his norm, and the possibility of understanding his own nature are all in God."[11] Created in the image of God, the human being sets himself in opposition to this origin. Thus, writes Brunner, "Man as sinner is in permanent revolt, in a rebellion (which he cannot now renounce by his own efforts) against his divine determination as intended in Creation, and against the nature given him by God."[12] It is this opposition to God that determines the contradiction in our nature, a conflict between our nature as intended by God and our actual nature.[13] Even when we are unaware of the true source of this conflict, we experience it as a conflict between what we actually are and what we ought to be.

Central to our experience of this conflict is the problem of human freedom. "The problem of freedom is peculiarly 'the' problem of human existence." This is so because "freedom is the original element of personal being. [It] is the specifically human characteristic."[14] In order to acknowledge that which is truly human, one must affirm human freedom. Without freedom, there is no responsibility and without responsibility, "the whole meaning of human existence disappears."[15]

Sin, says Brunner, is the opposite of freedom; it is unfreedom. Thus, we can understand the conflict of human experience as that between freedom and unfreedom. But we must clearly distinguish what Brunner means by these terms.

According to him, the Christian understanding of freedom must counter all forms of responsibility-denying determinism. It must also counter simultaneously what Brunner calls the *humanistic understanding of freedom*. Humanism rightly emphasizes that the human person is a subject, an "I," capable of responsible action. However, individual freedom tends to be absolutized. Freedom is thought to arise out of a person's individuality. While Brunner considers this to be superior to any form of determinism, it provides an inadequate Christian understanding of freedom.[16]

For Brunner, the Christian notion of freedom is "freedom-in-responsibility" and "freedom-in-and-for-love."[17] On the deepest level, the recognition of the relative and contingent character of our freedom is an acknowledgment of the dependent character of our being. Only God is absolute, thus only God's freedom may be absolutized. In contrast, human freedom is freedom-in-dependence: "The being of God alone is unconditioned, absolute freedom; that of the creature is conditioned, relative freedom, freedom in dependence."[18] In purely logical terms, this seems paradoxical, namely, that our freedom is derived from dependence upon God. But, since God is a person, he approaches human beings as persons. He addresses the human person's freedom and bestows upon him the responsibility of responding.

This responsibility has at least two meanings. The first refers to the usual meaning of the term where the individual is responsible for his freedom, choices, and consequences. Brunner notes that responsibility is often experienced as a burden; we cannot evade having to make choices in each moment of our lives. According to the second meaning, the call to responsibility is a call to love. Even the sinner must respond to God. Each person is called by God to love, and this call, Brunner argues, is unavoidably directed to our freedom at its deepest core. God does not coerce individuals into a loving relation with him. For the sinner, the experience of being called and answered is that of the law, of obligation, of the "thou-shalt-not." For the person who has turned to God, the call is revealed as one of love.

Brunner views sin as unfreedom. However, he is careful to distinguish this from any sort of determinism; the unfreedom of sin is brought about through our own decision, that is, through our freedom. According to Brunner, sin does not destroy our humanity, because it consists in our capacity for freedom: "free will is the presupposition and the essence of . . . human existence."[19] What does it mean to say that sin enslaves people? In the first place, Brunner argues, it refers to our condition of being incapable of not sinning (*non posse non peccare*). We are naturally inclined to sin, selfishness, and vice. We can never attain to a state in which we could no longer sin, a state in which we would be free from sin.

Hence the first meaning of unfreedom refers to the incapacity to be free from sin and hence the ever present predisposition toward vice and evil.

There is also a deeper meaning. It is not freedom as such that is lost through sin, but rather freedom in its deepest and ultimate sense that is based on "communion with God." By sinning, man "lives no longer in God but against him. He has been detached and alienated from his creator, the source of his life, from the Good, from love, which is his original life."[20] Because of sin, the human person has the hopeless task of squaring the circle: he has to do good before he is good; he has to aspire to God before he knows and loves God. He has to love God even though he is not in love with God. Just as a person who is no longer in water cannot swim, so a person who is no longer in love cannot love. Thus the loss of freedom in the sense of which Brunner speaks is not the freedom required to act out of one's self or even that required by virtue. Rather, it is the freedom to love God that has been lost. If a person can no longer "love as one loves in God," then he can no longer fulfill "the divine meaning of his life." He can no longer "fulfill that which gives to his life its genuinely human character."[21]

Karl Barth: Christological Anthropologist

Karl Barth (1886-1968) was formally schooled in the nineteenth-century Protestant liberal theology that he would eventually reject. In response to the crisis of European society following World War I, Barth considered his early theological reflection to be a "theology of crisis" and, like Brunner, to be a "dialectical theology." It rejected the idea that there is any natural point of contact between the Gospel and culture. God is outside of humanity's grasp. There is no human way to God; God seeks man, not man God. This situation leads to a crisis.

Barth criticized any human attempt to resolve the crisis, such as liberal Protestantism's uncritical accommodation with modern society. In contrast, Barth believed that theology must become radically theocentric. The fundamental axiom of Barth's theology is that God is God.

Barth's most mature statement of his theological anthropology occurs within the *Church Dogmatics*. The theological anthropology that emerges from Barth's analysis is radically Christocentric, with Jesus Christ being the measure of all humanity. It is the person of Christ who reveals the true nature of the human person. By virtue of our creation in God's image, humans are inextricably related to God. As a person himself, Christ sets the example of how to relate to other persons. Our freedom plays a central role in how we respond to God and to other persons. Our freedom is such that it is essentially a freedom for our response to God, for solidarity with others, and for personal communion.

The Christian Realism of Reinhold Niebuhr

Reinhold Niebuhr (1892-1971) is widely considered to be one of the most influential American theologians of the twentieth century. His theology developed in critical response to the prevailing social Darwinism, that is, the belief that society, according to its own inner dynamism, will continue to improve and advance materially, morally, and personally. Niebuhr reacted to the naive idealism of the Social Gospel Movement, the radical and typically socialist ideal of institutionalizing the Sermon on the Mount.

Niebuhr's theological anthropology received its definitive exposition in *The Nature and Destiny of Man*, first presented as the 1939 Gifford Lectures at the University of Edinburgh. Like Brunner, Niebuhr uses the paradoxical or contradictory character of human experience to introduce his anthropological reflections. He understands this paradox to arise from the fact that the human person is part of the natural order and a spiritual being capable of transcendence. He writes, "The obvious fact is that man is a child of nature, subject to its vicissitudes, compelled by its necessities, driven by its impulses, and confined within the brevity of years which nature permits its varied organic forms." The less obvious fact, Niebuhr contends, is that "man is a spirit who stands outside of nature, life, himself, his reason, and the world."[22] In more general terms, this conflict arises from the fact that the human being is both finite and free.

Our difficulty in comprehending this paradox finds expression throughout the history of ideas in the tendency to affirm one dimension of the human situation at the expense of another. That we are part of nature is presupposed in all forms of naturalism and materialism, yet the affirmation of this fact often leads to the denial of the human being's capacity for transcendence. However, all forms of rationalism and idealism tend to overemphasize the human capacities for transcendence (through reason and will) and forget our "relation to nature"[23] by identifying the person solely with the spiritual, divine, or eternal.

Transcendence is a central concept in Niebuhr's anthropology and requires elucidation. Broadly, it refers to the fact that as free beings we are capable of transcending our natural and social environments in order to transform them. It is possible to transcend nature while remaining subject to it.

Niebuhr accents the human capacity for self-transcendence. Humans often subject nature and society to rational analysis, thus leaving open the possibility of subjecting rational categories to criticism and question. Humans are capable of transcending their own rational categories, that is, moving beyond, reformulating, and criticizing them. Furthermore, persons frequently subject themselves to scrutiny and evaluation. What happens in these cases is that the self becomes the object of questioning, action, and manipulation.

Christianity not only affirms the contradiction of our freedom and finitude, it also recognizes that this situation is the precondition for a further contradiction introduced through human sinfulness. For Niebuhr, Christian theology insists that the problem of finitude is subordinate to the problem of sin:

> Man is a sinner. His sin is defined as rebellion against God. The Christian estimate of human evil is so serious precisely because it places evil at the very center of the human personality: in the will. This evil cannot be regarded complacently as the inevitable consequence of his finiteness or the fruit of his involvement in the contingencies and necessities of nature. Sin is occasioned precisely by the fact that man refuses to admit his creatureliness. He pretends to be more than he is.[24]

Niebuhr contends that the reality and seriousness of evil do not override human freedom. On the contrary, freedom presupposes evil: "Man contradicts himself within the terms of his own essence. His essence is for free self-determination. His sin is the wrong use of his freedom."[25]

Niebuhr argues that the tendency to sin in human nature is rooted in the conflict between freedom and finitude though it is neither identical with this conflict nor necessitated by it. As humans make themselves the center and source of their own lives, the human situation evidences contradictory theoretical and experiential tendencies. According to Niebuhr, the law of our nature is love, that is, "a harmonious relation of life to life in obedience to the divine center and source of life."[26] However, sin upsets this harmony.

The desire to overcome the conflict between our finitude and freedom leads in two divergent directions. On the one hand, it leads to the exertion of freedom to the point of denying our finitude and the contingent, dependent character of our existence (pride and self-love). On the other hand, it leads to the constriction of freedom or to immersion in sensuality.[27]

The conflict between our finitude and freedom expresses itself in anxiety. We experience ourselves as insecure and fragile. As part of nature, we experience our contingency, insecurity, and vulnerability; however, being free we can experience transcendence. Anxiety, Niebuhr argues, is the precondition for both sin and creativity. It is because we are insecure, ill at ease, or uncomfortable, that we attempt to overcome this situation. When done right, this leads to creative action. When done wrong, it leads to pride.

Niebuhr's analysis of pride (inordinate self-assertion) is particularly insightful. He distinguishes between the pride of power, knowledge, and virtue. The pride of power usually takes two forms. The first form arises from an extraordinary sense of self-control, which is then extended to control others. It is a pride in which the ego "assumes its self-sufficiency and self-mastery and imagines itself secure against all vicissitudes. It does not recognize the contingent and dependent character of its life and believes itself to be the author of its own existence, the judge of its own values, and the master of its own destiny."[28] The second form arises not from an extraordinary sense of self-mastery, but from the experience of insecurity. It becomes expressed in resentment, greed, and the temptation to regard security and comfort as the final and highest good.

Intellectual pride is expressed in the failure to recognize the finite, contingent character of human knowledge, while moral pride is "revealed in all 'self-righteous' judgments in which the other is condemned because he fails to conform to the highly arbitrary standards of the self."[29] Since the self engages in self-evaluation by its own standards, its results are favorable.

If left alone, this moral pride will eventually develop into a distinctively spiritual pride that consists in "making the self-deification implied in moral pride explicit."[30] Niebuhr argues that this form of pride manifests itself in individuals as well as in social groups, for example, in the forms of racism, nationalism, and the excessive competition among factions.

Niebuhr is perhaps best remembered for his Christian realism. Realism demands the universality of sin to be acknowledged, but it is not overly pessimistic. He writes, "A profound religion will not give itself to the illusion that perfect justice can be achieved in a sinful world. But neither can it afford to dismiss the problem of justice or to transcend it by premature appeals to the good will of individuals."[31] Realism means accepting the need for social and political structures or institutions that attempt to curb the excesses of human sin. Hence, human society requires some level of coercion.

Realism, however, recognizes the inevitable tension between striving for justice in the social order and maintaining freedom. Laws, which are necessarily coercive, are established so that individuals will not rapaciously take advantage of one another, being more concerned with their own weal than with that of others. This negative sense of justice and freedom is, for Niebuhr, the best possible approximation of love in social relations before the Parousia. "Even if perfect love were presupposed," he cautions, "complex relations, involving more than two persons, require the calculation of rights."[32] Realism means facing the inevitability of this tension while resisting either a naive optimism or a cynical pessimism.

Catholic Theology

Twentieth-century Catholic theology can be characterized in terms of three general movements: the theology of ressourcement, neo-Scholasticism, and transcendental Thomism. The first, associated with the names of Henri de Lubac, Jean Danielou, M. Chenu, and Yves Congar, consisted in a tremendous effort to recover the sources of the Christian faith, primarily through the study of the patristics. The purpose of the ressourcement theology was not a simple "going back" arising from a rejection of the contemporary situation. Rather, it consisted in the goal of "re-rooting" contemporary theology in its sources: in the reality of Christ and his actions and the church's experience of that reality throughout history. What united these various thinkers was "the double conviction that theology had to speak to the present situation, and that the condition for doing so faithfully lay in a recovery of the Church's past."[33] Thus, the aim of retrieving the past was to facilitate openness to the present and to enhance our understanding of the ways that Christian reality is experienced today. A brief presentation is given of Henri de Lubac's theological anthropology, particularly his recovery of the patristic sense of the unity of humanity.

The second movement considered is that of transcendental Thomism. Within German theology, transcendental Thomism has played an important role in the development of twentieth-century Catholic theology. Developed by such thinkers as J. Marèchal and P. Rousselot, the thrust of transcendental Thomism was to reexamine the philosophy of Thomas Aquinas in order to discover ways in which Thomistic philosophy could incorporate the genuine insights of transcendental thought. Karl Rahner, whose anthropology is considered briefly, extended the engagement of transcendental Thomism to the philosophy of Hegel and Heidegger.

The third movement is that of neo-Scholasticism. As with both transcendental Thomism and ressourcement theology, neo-Scholasticism also aimed at the systematic recovery of a part of the church's tradition that had been lost, not as a form of nostalgia, but with the purpose of bringing the riches of the past to bear on the present. In this case, Scholastic thought was recovered. Some prominent representatives of twentieth-century neo-Scholasticism are Etienne Gilson and Jacques Maritain. Though Maritain is, strictly speaking, a philosopher and not a theologian, his thought serves as a bridge to personalism, since he was loosely associated with the personalist movement in France and his thought influenced the development of personalism in Poland.

Henri de Lubac's Christian Humanism and the Common Destiny of Man

Among Henri de Lubac's most influential works, mention should be made of *Catholicism*, which recovered the patristic vision of humanity and the church as a community "rooted in the trinitarian concept of God."[34] His work *On the Supernatural* demonstrated the unity and continuity of the Catholic understanding of grace from the patristics through Thomas Aquinas. In a very different vein, *The Drama of Atheist Humanism* critically engaged the antitheistic philosophies of Feuerbach, Marx, Comte, and Nietzsche from the perspective of a Christian humanism. Our concern here is to indicate certain central theses from the first and last of these texts.

In *The Drama of Atheist Humanism*, de Lubac analyzes the humanistic philosophies of Feuerbach, Marx, Nietzsche, and Comte as essentially antitheistic, which was distinct from the more mundane atheistic humanism of lesser thinkers. Despite the differences among them, de Lubac argues that the fundamental pillar of the humanism that each espouses is the same, namely, the overt and radical rejection of God. This radical denial and rejection of God does not leave the concept of the human person unaffected. On the contrary, by denying the very foundation of the person's dignity and value, antitheistic humanism finally ends in the annihilation of the human person.[35]

This claim may seem paradoxical at first, since in many respects the principal motivation for declaring the "death of God" is the affirmation of the greatness of humanity and human freedom. The idea was that by freeing humanity from the concept of a supreme being humans would experience true freedom. For if there is no God, then the human being is sovereign. He becomes the creator and the source of "truth," "value," and "meaning." If there is no God, there is no universal moral law to which all humans must be subject. The "last bondage," says Nietzsche, is "the world of truth," since "truth" is nothing more than "the shadow of the dead God." If God is dead, then the reason, truth, and morality that owed their existence to him are "nothing but idols."[36] Without God, there are no limitations on what the human being can do except for the limitations he places upon himself.

This appeal to the greatness of humanity made possible by the death of God intoxicated hordes of people in this century, finding its most violent expression in fascism and Communism. The consequence of these ideological currents was not the elevation of human beings but their mass annihilation. Paradoxically, by elevating humanity to the level of God by supplanting God, antitheistic humanism removed the basis for recognizing the human being as anything more than raw material for "the preparation of some future society or for ensuring, here and now, the dominance of one privileged group." Within the framework of antitheism, there is nothing to prevent an individual person from being "cast aside as useless" or being systematically annihilated in the name of some greater cause or even in the name of personal ambition. What began as a lofty vision of the greatness of the human being ends by reducing him to a "mere cell completely merged in a mass," a mere tool used for furthering certain ends, an essentially disposable thing in which there is no "stability or depth" and no "value exacting universal respect."[37]

The Christian understanding of the person, while recognizing that the human person is subject to and dependent on God, does not end in devaluing the person. On the contrary, Christian humanism affirms the value and dignity of each and every person. In teaching that humans are made in God's image and destined for eternal life, Christianity reveals to the human person the greatness of her dignity and freedom. From the patristics, de Lubac recovers an original Christian humanism:

> O man, scorn not that which is admirable in you! You are a poor thing in your own eyes but I would teach you that in reality you are a great thing! The heavens have not been made in God's image as you have, nor the moon, nor the sun, nor

> anything to be seen in creation. Behold, of all that exists there is nothing that can contain your greatness.[38]

From the beginning of Christianity onward, this revelation of the dignity of the human person was seen as a great deliverance, since by it the human being was freed "in his own eyes, from the ontological slavery with which fate burdened him." Rather than being controlled by the necessary laws of nature, by the stars and the circle of life and death, the human being, each individual "had a direct link to the Creator, the Ruler of the stars themselves." The transcendent God, the friend of humanity, revealed in Jesus, "opened for all a way which nothing would ever bar again." It is this revelation of the dignity and liberty of the human person which, in de Lubac's words, accounts for the "intense feeling of gladness and of radiant newness to be found everywhere in early Christian writings."[39]

In our time this sense of the newness of the Christian vision has been lost. The dignity of the person and personal freedom that it reveals have become burdensome; the freedom that is liberty from sin, evil, and death has been trivialized into a simple capacity for choice. A recovery of the recognition of this dignity and the meaning of freedom is the necessary foundation for a genuinely Christian humanism: a humanism that neither denigrates human dignity and the greatness of human creativity, nor denies our inherent tendency toward vice, sin, and death. It is a humanism that recognizes our fundamental relation to God and members of the human community.

This brings us to a second dimension of de Lubac's theology; the essentially social or communal character of humanity that is revealed in Christianity. Referencing the patristic theologians, de Lubac demonstrates that in their vision the central Christian doctrines concerning the origin, condition, and destiny of the human person must be understood not only individually but also in terms of humanity as a whole. Just as each of us is made in the image of God, so are we united with one another in this image; just as through sin we become alienated from God, so our individual sins divide us from one another; just as Christ came to reestablish our union with the Father, so he came to make possible our unity with one another.

The church fathers argued that the image of God inhering in all humans unifies humanity, forming us into "one spiritual family intended to form one city of God."[40] It is because the image is "one" that we are all "one." Here the term *one* has two meanings. In the first place, it refers to the identity of the image, whereas in the second, it refers to the unity of all those formed by the image. Since the image in each of us is the source of our unity with one another, any "infidelity to the divine image" is at the same time "a disruption of human unity."[41] Sin is essentially a division, a separation, a "breaking up." It causes both internal and social disruption. Sin destroys God's desire for human unity by turning us into "a multiple of individuals, as numerous as the sands of the seashore," with each of us suffering from "violently discordant inclinations."[42]

Through his Incarnation and atonement, Jesus Christ unites humanity. The disunity caused by sin can only be overcome through the grace of redemption.[43] We must maintain a proper understanding of the unity of humanity. It is not a unity of being that swallows individuality. Rather, it is a unity that presupposes our unique individuality. To express this truth, early Christian theologians often employed the image of a harmonious symphony, in which each individual member must contribute in its distinctiveness in order to form a whole.[44]

Though this essentially communal dimension of the human person seems foreign to our modern emphasis on the person as a radically unique individual, de Lubac argues that it is essentially compatible with a right understanding of the individual. Indeed, the recovery of the communal dimension of the person is a necessary antidote to the modern tendency to affirm an atomistic individualism—an individualism that views the person as radically autonomous and independent of others and denies the significance of personal relations of obligation, dependence, solidarity, and love.

Karl Rahner and the Notion of Christian Freedom

Though Karl Rahner wrote a number of systematic theological works—*Spirit in the World*, *Hearers of the Word*, and *Foundations of the Christian Faith*—much of his theology was developed in essays, and it is from these that we draw his theology of freedom.

According to Rahner, Christian freedom is nothing but a genuine "human freedom," granted by God to every human being as "a dignity, a task and an inescapable burden."[45] From Christian theology we know that this freedom is not simply a capacity or power to choose among finite objects or finite courses of action. Freedom is born of the "transcendence" of the human being, that is, the human being's capacity for, and relation to, the absolute and infinite being. Thus, whether we know or experience it, our freedom is essentially "freedom before and towards God."[46] Rahner not only refers to freedom as our capacity to accept or to reject God in any concrete individual instance. It is the very nature of freedom that whenever we act freely we are also acting before God and in relation to him. God is not one object among others that may or may not be chosen; God is the "infinite horizon" that makes every free act possible.

Since human freedom situates us in relation to the eternal God, it is the ultimate ground of our dignity. Freedom is also, as Rahner says, a task and a burden. We do not understand it rightly if we think of freedom simply as the power to choose. Freedom must be realized; it is a task and a demand. As persons, God continually calls us to be free, to form ourselves as free, responsible beings. Thus freedom, in this sense, cannot be understood negatively as simply the absence of external constraint. As human persons, we are by essence free spiritual subjects who act in relation to God and to others. We cannot escape our freedom, even when we try to submerge ourselves in immanent drives and impulses or lose ourselves in external forces and events. We must determine ourselves as free beings and therefore in relation to God. It is for this reason that freedom can often be experienced as a burden.

Since freedom is a task to be realized, we can distinguish a genuine and authentic freedom from a false, distorted freedom. Rahner analyzes genuine freedom in terms of five elements or dimensions. In the first place, a genuine freedom is one that recognizes its finitude. To put it another way, the person who is genuinely free recognizes the limitations of his or her condition as a finite human being and with that, the limitations of his or her freedom. These limitations include the limitations of nature (e.g., that we are bodily beings subject to biological and physiological laws) and the limitations of the concrete, historical situation in which we find ourselves.

We can respond to the fact of our finitude in two general ways: We can either stubbornly rebel against it or try to deny it, or we can freely accept this situation and claim responsibility for our actions. In saying that we accept our limitations, Rahner does not mean that we must simply resign ourselves to the status quo. It is also a genuine dimension of human freedom to be creative and open to new possibilities. The great technological advances that characterize our culture are an expression of the desire to free ourselves from limitations and to push the boundaries of the possible in the realm of nature (the possibilities opened up through genetic engineering demonstrate the extraordinary extent of this desire). However, Rahner points out, technology itself is something to which we can become subordinate. We run the risk of replacing, in a sense, the necessities of nature with those of technology, and it is undoubtedly the case that technological advances can also immensely increase the compulsive powers of institutions, governments, and organizations.[47] The point to be kept in mind is a formal but extremely significant one; as human beings we are essentially finite and limited, and a genuine freedom recognizes this existential fact.

In the second place, a genuine freedom is formed by the "will to truth." A genuine freedom is not one that is arbitrary, driven by subjective desires and impulses and guided solely by subjective, uninformed opinion. The will to truth, Rahner says, especially frees us from the "interior dangers" that threaten genuine freedom even more than external factors and conditions. These interior dangers consist in our own shortsightedness, pride, and blinding egoism.[48] These habits of the heart can cripple freedom and make us incapable of responding effectively to the world around us through responsible freedom. Their corrective includes a capacity for self-criticism, the courage to allow oneself to be taught, a willingness to listen to others, and a commitment to searching for objective standards. The will to truth is part of the hard work and struggle of achieving a genuine freedom.

The third dimension of a genuine freedom is that it respects the freedom of others. This respect consists negatively in a tolerance for others, and positively in an active desire to seek open dialogue with others.[49] Genuine freedom is thus opposed to any and all forms of compulsion, control, and domination. It is committed to the difficult tasks of genuine dialogue—making oneself known to others and coming to know them, even when the exchange is painful and difficult. Thus, respect for others cannot be conceived of simply as a "letting others be." It is a respect that manifests itself in the desire to understand others and to find common ground with them so as to form genuine communities of persons.

The fourth element of a genuine freedom is the "courage to risk the unforeseeable future," it is a freedom of "creative hope" that anticipates the "new things which are both one's own and unexpected and unplanned."[50] This fourth dimension is the correlate to the first mentioned above; the recognition of our finitude must be accompanied by an understanding of the creativity of freedom and the courage to be open to change and the future. It is not, however, a blind, naive optimism. It is a responsible openness that demands "knowledge, reflection, [and] circumspection," and it is not blind since its ultimate basis is a hope in the infinite, transcendent God who opens up the future to us.[51]

The fifth and final element of genuine freedom consists in the recognition that the ultimate achievement of freedom "is the unique event of the personal uniqueness of every [human being] in his finality before God." This is, Rahner says, the ultimate nature and mystery of freedom; each of us as an individual stands before God and is both capable of responding and required to respond to God with our whole being. It is the final and ultimate commitment of the spiritual subject: "acceptance or rejection of him who is the incomprehensible love."[52] The paradox of freedom is present here. God is the condition of the possibility of human freedom, and yet with that freedom we can reject him.[53] The ultimate nature of our freedom also constitutes our highest dignity and, indeed, constitutes our dignity as eternal even though we are finite, for in our freedom, we face the eternal being and accept or reject him. Here we see both the grandeur of freedom and also its terrible and eternal burden.

Jacques Maritain: The Person and Society

Among the fundamental problems confronting any anthropology, theological or philosophical, the problem of rightly understanding the relation between the individual person and society is crucial. Jacques Maritain devoted many works to this subject including *The Person and the Common Good, Freedom in the Modern World, The Rights of Man*, and *The Natural Law*.

There are two errors to be avoided in conceptualizing the relation between the individual person and society. On the one hand, one must affirm the independence and "totality" of the person over and against every form of totalitarianism that absorbs the individual person into a larger whole, conceiving of the individual as one cell in a larger organism. On the other hand, one must avoid so exaggerating the independence and "totality" of the individual person that one conceives of society as simply the aggregate of individual wills, an "anarchy of atoms."[54]

To understand the distinction and relation between the individual person and society, Maritain distinguishes between (1) the terms *person* and *individual*, (2) the relation of individual good and common good, (3) freedom as a conquest, and (4) a society of free persons.

Theological Anthropology and Personalism

The Development of Personalism

Economic personalism synthesizes the contributions of three twentieth-century European traditions of personalism—the French, German, and Polish schools.[55] The genesis of personalism can be found in an increasing awareness of human dignity and the interest in the dynamics of personal existence. Its central question is: What does it mean to be a person? Personalism analyzes the meaning and nature of personal existence. Yet it recognizes that no theory could ever fully explain and define the intricate dynamic that is human life. The human person is a complex subject, and the depths of subjectivity within the individual human person know no limits.

Many of the developments of personalism derive from theological anthropology. Christian theologians, both Protestant and Catholic, have reflected on the mystery of humanity. Questions of sin and grace, the nature of God and man, and redemption have all led to the gradual formulation of a Christian anthropology. Many of their insights have been incorporated into the works of various personalists. However, personalism has its own distinct philosophical traditions as well. It would be acceptable to speak of personalism as divided into three basic branches or types: French, German, and Polish. This is not to exclude the American variants, but for the purpose of this work, American personalism is not included. We believe that it is the European forms of personalism that have the most to offer this project.

The scope of this work prevents a detailed exposition and analysis of all personalist thinkers and theories. For the sake of brevity, we highlight only the central thinkers of each strand of personalism and briefly describe their contributions. Such an exposition—though introductory—will still enrich our discussion. It is our aim to combine theological anthropology with personalist insights in order to convey a coherent Christian vision of the human person.

French Personalism

Emphasis on the nature and value of the human person has not been confined to any school or group in recent French philosophy. Philosophical reflection on the personal aspects of existence—relationships, love, faith, and human nature—can be found in the works of several French philosophers.

Beginning with Descartes's analysis of personal consciousness through Bergson's vitalism, we see French thinkers taking up issues related to philosophical anthropology. Even the French Thomist revival had Maritain discussing the person in relation to rights, the state, and community. However, when one thinks of personalism as a particular type or style of French philosophy, two thinkers strongly recommend themselves: Emmanuel Mounier (1905-1950) and Gabriel Marcel (1889-1973).

Emmanuel Mounier

In the midst of a crisis that pervaded every area of French life in the early 1930s, a new generation of French citizens came of age. The new generation believed that the values, the ideas, and the structures of the society of their elders were important in resolving the crisis. In various journals the youth of France voiced its criticism of the status quo and elaborated its programs of revolutionary change. The very titles that members gave their journals suggested what one of them was to call in a classic phrase, "the established disorder." Among the new journals were *L'Ordre Nouveau*, *L'Homme Nouveau*, *La Revue des Vivants*, and *Esprit*. Of these journals only one was to survive the 1930s and influence future generations of French thought—*Esprit*. It became one of the most acclaimed journals in France.

The monthly *Esprit* was founded by Emmanuel Mounier. Educated at Grenoble and the Sorbonne, Mounier went on to become a professor of philosophy, a position he held for many years. Mounier, however, was dissatisfied with the academic culture of his time finding it excessively removed from current-day affairs. Even after enlivening his own teaching style, permitting interruptions and encouraging class debate, Mounier found academic life unrewarding. This lack of satisfaction led him to engage the crisis of his times by launching the journal.

Mounier always had a fascination with those areas of philosophy that were practical, or more specifically, could be called existential. Focusing on the work of the existentialists, Mounier developed his own style of philosophical anthropology and reflection called personalism. Mounier's personalism had as its purpose not to dominate, not to provide definitive solutions, but rather to serve, to raise questions, to challenge comfortable assumptions, to act as a catalyst in the making of personal decisions.

This unsystematic approach was inspired by the work of Charles Peguy. Mounier joined Peguy in denouncing ready-made and closed philosophical systems, any sort of secluded and abstract intellectualizing, and the morally debilitating effects of comfortable intellectual habits.

Mounier's *Revolution Personnaliste et Communautaire* first appeared in 1935. This unsystematic attempt to elaborate a personalism brought much attention to the work of *Esprit* as well. A year later he published *Manifesto au Service du Personnalisme*. This work outlined suggestions for changing the general structures of society to better respect the dignity of man.

Mounier was a deeply committed Christian, yet humble in the face of the convictions and beliefs of others. While the final end of man lay in the next world, Mounier still believed that it was essential to work for a better here and now. Persons must bear witness to the eternal verities by committing themselves in the temporal affairs of their time.

Mounier took positions that were critical of the market, liberal democracy, fascism, and the bourgeois spirit of his day. He resisted any political movements that restricted human liberty or attempted to subsume the person into some sort of collective scheme. *Esprit* and Mounier's early works took radical stances of pacifism, anti-Francoism, anticommunism, and antinationalism. As early as 1935 he condemned France's actions in Indo-China. With the outbreak of World War II, Mounier was devastated. He watched the horror unfold and witnessed the collapse of his nation. Reluctantly, and only out of the deepest opposition to the Nazis, he joined the Resistance. His efforts earned him the suppression of *Esprit* and imprisonment by the Vichy regime.

After the war Mounier revived *Esprit* and continued with his critique of contemporary culture. His calls for social reform did not leave the church immune either. He chastised Christianity and the Roman Catholic Church for "becoming conservative, defensive, sulky, and afraid of the future." He continued his attacks on socialism, Communism, and nationalism, always defending human liberty and railing against collectivism in all its forms. Shortly before his death Mounier commented:

> Insofar as it depends on me, personalism will never be either a system or a political machine. We find the word useful to describe a certain outlook on human problems and to accentuate certain demands which do not always receive sufficient consideration in proposed solutions for our present crises.[56]

Mounier's final exposition of personalism was his best received, entitled *Personalism*. Due to his intentionally unsystematic approach it is difficult to outline this work. However, we endeavor to draw out several themes that Mounier develops throughout the book.

Mounier saw personalism as a philosophy whose central affirmation was the freedom and creativity of persons. Mounier warned against beginning personalist reflection with definitions of the person. One can aptly define objects exterior to man, but the subjectivity of another is a different matter. If one takes the example of a friend, one begins to understand this difficulty. You can examine your friend's appearance and not fully comprehend him. You can evaluate him psychologically, engage him in analysis, or perform a battery of tests. You can classify him according to various criteria: He is Protestant, a Frenchman, of the middle class, and so on. You can even name him. Yet, in the thousands of ways in which we can distinguish him, we do not exhaust his being, we do not fully embrace, nor understand, his personhood. We encounter him and cannot fully explain him.

This sense of the mystery of my neighbor does not mean that we cannot speak intelligently about him, or differentiate him from other things. This is the mystery of personhood. We experience it since we are persons, we encounter it in other persons, yet we cannot fully explain it ourselves:

> But the essence of the person, being indefinable, is never exhausted by its expression, nor subjected to anything by which it is conditioned. Nor is it definable as some internal substratum as a substance lurking underneath our attitudes, an abstract principle of our overt behavior. It is the living activity of self-creation, of communication, and of attachment, that grasps and knows itself, in the act, as the movement of becoming personal.[57]

However, Mounier did not think that nothing could be said about the person. Although no definition of the person is fully adequate, descriptions can begin to approximate personal being. Mounier offered this description in the *Manifesto*:

> Man is a body in the same degree that he is a spirit, wholly body wholly spirit.... Man is a natural being: by his body he is a part of nature and the body is everywhere with him.... Man is a natural being. But is he no more than that? Is he altogether a sport of nature? Or does he, plunged into and emerging out of nature, transcend it?[58]

According to Mounier, philosophy had for the most part ignored the person until the twentieth century. The early Greeks had been more fascinated by the cosmos and the natural order than by human beings. The Greek worldview continued through the Roman era, but changed with the advent of Christianity. With the Incarnation came the focus on the human being. God acted so as to redeem human persons, not merely the natural order, or some abstract cosmos.

Yet, Mounier points out, even Christianity did not fully appreciate the person immediately. Even through the Scholastics we see a continued fixation on nonpersonal being. The concept of the person had been elucidated by the Trinitarian and Christological controversies, but, according to Mounier, the

Greek intellectual framework was still so heavily relied upon as to stymie the expression of the person in adequate terms.

Philosophy turns markedly away from the person with Hegel. Hegel's systemization of philosophy reduced the person to a mere plaything of the dialectic. Humans were accidental properties of an unfolding cosmic order. Ethics was simply ignored in Hegel's abstract philosophizing. Historically speaking, existentialism and personalism arose in response to Hegel's abstract system building and armchair metaphysics. Mounier, therefore, understood personalism as a reaction against the excesses of the philosophy of ideas and the philosophy of things.

Gabriel Marcel

Marcel has often been classified as a Catholic existentialist. This label was given him by compatriot Jean Paul Sartre. Yet Marcel did not consider himself an existentialist; he thought of himself as a philosopher of the person. Born in Paris in 1889, Marcel studied in private schools throughout his early life, and later studied philosophy at the Sorbonne. He shared Mounier's dislike for Hegel and for abstract philosophy removed from the everyday world. He also shared Mounier's penchant for doing unsystematic philosophy.

Denied military service due to poor health, Marcel served in the Red Cross during World War I. As a Red Cross liaison Marcel represented families attempting to find or contact lost loved ones. In his job he was constantly besieged by distraught parents, wives, families, and lovers. Marcel tirelessly attempted to locate missing soldiers or even to gain accurate information concerning their fate. Often he was the one who first told of a loved one's death. These experiences profoundly shaped the thought of this young and sensitive soul.

He published the *Journal* in 1927. This work appeared in the form of a journal he kept from 1914 through 1923. In this short work he lays out the themes typical to existentialist writers: intersubjectivity, commitment, authentic living, the meaning of death, and so on. He converted to Catholicism in 1929 after being raised in an agnostic home. Faith, religion, duty, and the meaning of death and the afterlife all play a large role in his reflections. He was convinced until his death that secularization ultimately led to a materialism that denigrated humanity. Without the transcendent values of Christian faith, human existence is fractured by nature.

In 1933 Marcel published a play entitled *The Broken World* (*Le Monde Casse*). This play with a concluding philosophical postscript describes the tragedy of what Marcel termed the *functionalization of man*. Functionalization occurs when the individual begins to appear to himself and others as no more than a mere conglomeration of functions. Instead of viewing the person as a whole, as a mystery, he is reduced to a series of social functions. These functions, while a real facet of human identity, tended to be taken as the entirety of his identity in certain circles, especially the social sciences. So, rather than man the mystery, we have man the consumer, man the churchgoer, the ticket collector, the parent, the producer, and so on. The result is that the person is fragmented.

In such a functionalized world, mystery is lost. Life is viewed as a series of functions and problems. Indeed, Marcel makes a famous distinction between mystery and problem. While admitting that there are not exact lines of demarcation, Marcel defines a problem as a question whose answer, though difficult to obtain, is, in theory, obtainable. A problem does not fall outside the scope of human intellect. A mystery, on the other hand, is a question whose answer will never be fully provided. Mystery goes beyond the ability of the human intellect to comprehend fully. Marcel believes that the person and the things that can be rightly described as personal are mysteries.

Marcel provides the example of love as a mystery. John and Mary love one another. They think of each other, but they do not, let us suppose, think of love in any abstract way. There is simply the concrete union of mutual love between them. Suppose one of the partners steps back and attempts to analyze what love is. While intelligent thoughts may be offered about the subject, and while the subject matter is being experienced by both parties, neither will be able to provide a fully adequate answer to this query.

Indeed, love was a theme Marcel reflected on at great length. For him it provided the remedy to the functionalization of the secular world. In the desire to give oneself away to another we find ourselves, and are brought back to ourselves whole. Love is the epitome of the antifunctionalist mentality because it refuses to reduce the other to a series of tasks and performances. In genuine love the whole being of the other is appreciated rather than just particular aspects.

Summary of French Themes

It is impossible to do justice to the works of Mounier and Marcel in a few short pages. Their backgrounds have been presented and their general themes discussed. What can we conclude from this initial presentation?

French personalism was concerned with avoiding reductionism when it came to studying the human person. These thinkers are united in their resistance to twentieth-century trends that focus narrowly on one aspect or element of human existence to the exclusion of others. The person is, therefore, often depicted as a "nothing but ..." with various disciplines and ideologies filling in the blank.

French personalism strongly desired to depict the whole person in all of his or her mystery. Mounier and Marcel, both realizing the limitations of their efforts, desired to combat reductionism in all its forms. The antireductionistic attitude was the starting point for developing a body of thought that expounded upon the complexity of personal existence while affirming human dignity.

German Personalism

It is more accurate to speak of German philosophers who analyzed aspects of the human person than to speak of a tradition of German personalism. Existentialism and personalism never captured the imagination of German thinkers as it did the French intellectuals. Two German thinkers who did devote attention to specifically personalist issues were Max Scheler and Martin Buber. Scheler is considered a phenomenologist while Buber is usually classified as an existentialist. Both thinkers developed detailed anthropologies and even went on to apply their anthropological insights to the social problems of their day.

Max Scheler

Max Scheler (1874-1928) was part of the early phenomenological movement begun by Husserl and Reinach at the turn of the century. Scheler was a brilliant thinker, and his work covers an array of philosophical topics. He can be understood as having gone through three phases or periods in his work: (1) a neo-Kantian phase inspired by his early teacher Rudolf Eucken, (2) a Christian phenomenological period emphasizing ethical, aesthetic, and value philosophy, and (3) a final period of pantheism and inclination toward evolutionary naturalism not unlike Bergson's position.

Influenced by Husserl and his early students, Scheler developed his own variant of phenomenology, understanding it as an attitude of entering into an immediate relationship with an object. By philosophical anthropology Scheler meant philosophy as it applies to man, to his place in the world and in society, which also included value philosophy. During the middle period of his philosophical work, he conceived of man's proper function in the cosmos as one of modeling himself after God in terms of spiritual and religious values, emphasizing love and the dignity of the person. Scheler developed a value personalism in order to give concrete status to other abstract values. In his personalist philosophy, values are concretized in the person as the bearer of values. He later turned away in the direction of a Darwinian blend of Bergson and Freud.

Like Husserl, Scheler was influenced by the ideas of Brentano, particularly in developing the concept of ethical sanction that affirmed man's ability to discern good and evil by immediate apprehension. Man's a priori ability to gain insight intuitively into the structure of moral values is more than a pure intellectual function. Accepting Pascal's dictum that "the heart has its reason that the mind does not know," Scheler concluded that there is an order of the heart, or logic of the heart comparable to that of the intellect. In contrast to the Kantian view of moral values as rational, formal standards, he believed such values possess a material content that becomes immediately known to the individual through a process of intuition.

Values are of central importance in Scheler's ethics, but this does not mean that the person is subservient to a system of abstract values. To describe Scheler's moral philosophy as an ethics of abstract values is incorrect. It would be more accurate to characterize it as a value personalism. A concern for ethical a priori truths had led Scheler to an abstract concept of values. In order to overcome extreme abstraction and to regain the concrete, Scheler developed thoughts on personalism. Values were now seen as concretized or incarnated in the person, the bearer of values.

Love plays the role of discoverer in our perception of values. Love is a movement in the course of which new and higher values flash forth and reveal themselves, values hitherto unknown to the person. Hence, love does not follow after value feeling or value preference, but precedes them as their pioneer and leader.

> In living an act of pure love toward a person, the value of this person is detached from all simultaneously felt value-levels of our own personal world of values when we experience these as connected with our sense and feeling of life. . . . This value is also quite independent of any estimative deliberation about the permanence that an act of pure loving may have through happiness and sorrow, the inherent or accidental fate of life.[59]

In the book, *On the Eternal in Man*, Scheler establishes two constitutive marks of man: self-transcendence and an unceasing dynamic movement. Man is essentially a being that transcends itself.

> The attempted moral upsurge of the whole mental man is always simultaneously man's attempt to transcend himself as a finite being . . . an essential feature of the upsurge we are examining is the constant endeavor actually to detach one's own mental act-center from the psycho-physical nexus of human biology . . . and to transpose it into the universal act-center corresponding to the idea of God, so that from the vantagepoint and, so to speak, "in" the strength of that center one may look upon the being of all things.[60]

Not all personalists viewed Scheler as working on a common project. It is regrettable that even Mounier should have misinterpreted the value personalism of Scheler. In *Personalism*, Mounier comments, "Several contemporary thinkers (Scheler, Hartmann) speak of values, conceived as realities in themselves apart from their relations, and recognizable *a priori*. Personalists, however, cannot willingly surrender the person to anything impersonal, and most of them seek in one way or another to personalize these values."[61]

Hans Urs von Balthasar helpfully explains Scheler's personalism in terms of his struggle to overcome two philosophical positions of his time. First, he wanted to overcome the *Lebensphilosophie* of Nietzsche and Bergson. These two thinkers portrayed the essential aspect of man as spirit, or life principle, yearning to transform the material and social conditions of humanity. Second, he wanted to overcome German idealism insofar as it dissolved the individual into a mere instance of the universe. He teaches that the recognition of the infinite worth of the individual human soul is the magna carta of Europe.

A striking expression of Scheler's personalism is his understanding of the individual value-essence of each human person. He teaches that each person not only instantiates the general essence of man, but also has an essence incommunicably his own. The ethical consequence is that each person not only has to act on maxims that are universal laws for all persons, but also on maxims that bind him alone and no one else.

His understanding of the importance of the individual did not exclude the possibility of community. Scheler's personalism rather affirmed the social nature of the person. Still, he rejected any social philosophy that viewed the high point of human existence in collective living. Human community is something more discovered than created.

Scheler's sense of solidarity is not that of the mass or the crowd but of concrete individual persons. Therefore, Scheler's sense of solidarity is not reductionistic or collectivist. The individual does not derive his dignity from any other individual or any community. This also leads Scheler to note that each person is a whole of his own and is so strong as being of his own that no possible whole could ever encompass him as a mere part of itself.

On these grounds Scheler rejected nationalism and rather expounded the ideals of a Christian solidarism as the foundation for European cooperation and unity. He presented Christian solidarism as a golden mean between the extreme individualism of capitalism and the collectivism of socialism. Pointing to the community-building potential of Catholicism, Scheler made European Catholics aware of their social responsibility.

Martin Buber

Born in Vienna to a Jewish family in 1878, Martin Buber was educated at the University of Vienna and later at the University of Berlin. He received his doctorate in philosophy in 1904. After his philosophical studies he devoted the next five years to rabbinical studies and Jewish theology. Buber always desired to have his theological and philosophical training brought to bear on practical problems. He launched a periodical called *Der Jude* in 1916, and later, from 1926 to 1930, formed a partnership with Protestant and Catholic thinkers through the journal *Die Kreatur*, which was devoted to social issues of the day.

In 1920, Buber, in conjunction with others, established the Free Jewish Academy in Frankfurt. For the next ten years the academy tutored thousands of students in Jewish history, biblical studies, and Jewish literature. From 1923 to 1933 Buber held the chair of philosophy of religion and history of religions at the University of Frankfurt. When the Nazis rose to power in the early 1930s Buber was removed from his chair. In 1938, just in time to escape the Nazi persecutions, Buber went to Palestine to become professor of social philosophy at the Hebrew University in Jerusalem.

Buber's personalism revolves around the person and his relationship to others in community. In his essay *What Is Man?* Buber discusses what he believed to be the two primary social and anthropological errors of the modern age, namely, collectivism and individualism.

As Buber understands it, individualism sees man only in relation to himself. Yet, collectivism does not see man at all but only society. The errors of both views are the same, a misunderstanding of man and his place in the universe. Individualism reduces man to a solitary figure devoid of a social nature, while collectivism reduces man to a part of some organic whole, forgetting the substantiality of the individual.

In place of these inadequate social views, Buber offers community as the correct middle ground. Community is the totality of I-Thou relationships in which individuals live with and for others. Buber's chief insight in the book *I and Thou* is that there are two fundamental attitudes or postures to be found in all human experience. These may be called personal and functional. The personal treats another in relation to self as a thou or person, while the functional reduces the personhood of the other to an it. Buber continues by stating that repeated exposure to the I-it relationship eventually changes the I as well.

Relations with others is, therefore, a fundamental aspect of human development and flourishing. Buber states that the only way in which I can exercise a genuine existence is by engaging myself in a truly interpersonal relationship with the other. We cannot stand alone as I nor be consumed in the We. We must interact with one another as individuals who remain open to one another's contributions. Therefore, most properly, a genuine relationship is a relationship of I-Thou. The totality of these relationships forms the solidarity of community.

With the rapid advances of modern science and technology there is a growing tendency to consider man as less than a human being or genuine thou. More often man is reduced in impersonal ways to a number, a statistic, or an anonymous unit in a highly organized system. There is less and less attention paid to him as person. Buber clearly admits that we cannot, nor should not, roll back the technological advances. In many ways technology demonstrates human dignity as it depersonalizes man. Rather, we must learn how to live with technology while preserving the personal.

Summary of German Themes

Both Buber and Scheler understood the centrality and dignity of the individual human person. They took this recognition and applied it to social philosophy.

Their foundational question was: What is man's relationship to others? While both thinkers highly valued humanity's social nature, they refused to accept either collectivism or individualism. Both tendencies in social philosophy committed anthropological errors and were reductionistic. Rather than radical individualism or the hive mentality of the collective, Buber and Scheler sought after genuine community. Buber, more so than Scheler, works out a philosophical schema for genuine community. His explication of the I-Thou structure of community harmonizes with Scheler's thoughts on solidarity. The work of both thinkers would be instrumental in the development of personalism in Poland.

The Synthesis of Polish Personalism

Polish personalism, sometimes referred to as the Lublin School (founded in Lublin, Poland), was greatly influenced by both the phenomenological personalism of Scheler and the nonsystematic work of Mounier. Yet we find elements of all of the above thinkers in Polish personalism.

After World War II numerous Polish Catholic intellectuals were inspired by the work of the French personalists as found in *Esprit*. While the work of Maritain, Marcel, and Mounier was known in Poland prior to the war, it did not begin to bear fruit until after 1945. Carried on by thinkers such as Roman Ingarden and Karol Wojtyla, personalism slowly took root.

Poland, having been ravaged by the war and now under Communist rule, had several competing social theories vying for its national soul. The Marxist/Leninist social philosophy found Catholic Poland unfruitful soil. Thomism and other traditional Catholic intellectual frameworks had permeated Poland and its universities. Yet even Thomism failed to inspire this new generation of thinkers.

The central thinker in Polish personalism is Karol Wojtyla, also known as Pope John Paul II. Karol Wojtyla set out to analyze the ethics and anthropology of Max Scheler. This young priest wrote his doctoral dissertation assessing Scheler's views on morality and man. This study significantly affected his own understanding, and he began to lay out a new school of philosophical anthropology.

Wojtyla approached Scheler from the Thomistic foundation learned in his earlier theological training. In phenomenology, he found a new method of understanding the person from the perspective of action and experience. Using the new tools of phenomenology, Wojtyla was able to rethink many aspects of personal being.[62] While Thomism emphasized personal existence as more or less static rational substance, Scheler and his fellow thinkers developed the foundations of an anthropology of acting man.

Wojtyla seems to have focused special attention on French philosophical anthropology. Indeed, Wojtyla drew heavily from the personalism of Mounier and his fellow members of *Esprit*. Wojtyla and his Polish colleagues read Mounier with intense interest. In Mounier they found the first philosophical accounts of not only the human intellect but also of some other aspects of the soul, including affectivity and intersubjectivity.[63]

Wojtyla eventually came to teach philosophy at the Catholic University of Lublin, where he and his students developed the detailed core of Polish personalism. According to Wojtyla, analysis of the acting person can provide the starting point for all philosophizing. Subjects include human subjectivity and autonomy, the recognition of human dignity, elaboration of a theory of human rights, understanding of intersubjectivity, and all attempts to understand the ontological status of the acting person in his or her fullness: body and soul, mind, heart, and will—in this world but destined for another.

The most important book by Karol Wojtyla is *Osoba i Czyn* (Cracow, 1969), translated in a completely revised, definitive edition as *The Acting Person* (Dordrecht and Hingham, Massachusetts, 1979), the English version appearing in Holland and the United States after the author had become pope and without his having been able fully to control "the second half of the book" in its final reworking. As a decade separates these two publications, it would seem useful to regard them separately.

Wojtyla will later rely on his theological training as he builds his anthropology:

> We particularly want to explain what man is and what he must do in the light of this theological anthropology. Here we must begin by listening to what revelation tells us about man and by studying the basic structure of morality in the Bible (e.g., its religious response, its christocentrism, its salvation history and its eschatology); we might then discover how much these structures correspond to the a priori and transcendental understanding that contemporary man has of himself. It should incorporate the findings of the positive sciences, such as sociology, biology, psychology and medicine. These findings, critically examined, must be embodied in the image of man so that the Christian ethos will not be overlaid by secularization and relativism. Only in Christ can the world be saved in its totality.[64]

The position of humanity in the cosmos also requires a careful examination of the relation between our personal situation and the reality of creation as a whole.

If we clearly understand the meaning of "creature," we must make a clear distinction between the immanent contents of human existence and humanity's essential, transcendental relation to God. Although these two cannot be separated, they do not mean the same thing but explain each other. This distinction might be useful in reaching a better understanding of the disintegration caused in human beings and the world through sin, and the consequences of this fact on human action. God's Incarnation confirmed the reality of the creation. It also shows that humanity is essentially related to God, which is important for salvation history, because it implies that humanity must be integrated in salvation and be delivered from the powers of evil. It is thought that the validity of a natural moral law in the order of salvation and the question of a religious practice, which is turned toward the world, must be discussed in light of these principles.[65]

> If we celebrate with such solemnity the birth of Jesus, it is to bear witness that every human being is somebody unique and unrepeatable. If our human statistics, human categories, human political, economic and social systems, and mere human possibilities fail to ensure that man can be born, live and act as one who is unique and unrepeatable, then all this is ensured by God. For God and before God, the human being is always unique . . . somebody thought of and chosen from eternity, someone called and identified by his own name. . . . [I]t is humanity that is elevated in God's earthly birth. Humanity, human "nature" is taken into the unity of the divine Person of the Son. . . . The birth of the Incarnate Word is the beginning of a new power for humanity itself, a power open to every man . . . "to become children of God" (John 1:12). . . . Accept the great truth concerning man. . . . Accept the mystery in which every human being lives since Christ was born.[66]

Christ is not only a revelation of God and his salvific will for all mankind through the church but also a revelation of man, of what man was intended to be at creation and is by reason of the Incarnation of the Son of God and by reason of the Crucifixion, Resurrection, and Ascension of the God–Man Jesus Christ. It is quite probable that the pontiff's thought has not yet been fully presented to his own satisfaction in any one document. He makes cross-references, but even these do not wholly satisfy one trying to round out the whole meaning of what may be taken as a mainspring of his faith and action.[67]

> Christ—allow me to put it this way—is the greatest realist in the history of man. . . . It is precisely by virtue of this realism that Christ bears witness to the Father and bears witness to man. He Himself, in fact, knows "what is in man" (Jn. 2:25). He knows! . . . And precisely the basis of this realism, Christ teaches that human life has meaning insofar as it is a testimony of truth and love.[68]

The hallmark of Wojtyla's personalistic method is the conviction that the potential to participate is a part of the self. It is obvious that this potential has to be activated, formed, and cultivated in order to bring about its fullest realization. "Man lives and acts with others not only because it is his nature to do so, but also because in this acting and being 'jointly with others' he can reach his level of maturity . . . the level of maturity of the self."[69] For this reason one has to recognize everyone's fundamental right to act and thus everyone's freedom to act, through the exercise of which the self fulfills itself. The meaning of this right and of this freedom is contained in the personalistic value of the human act. On the basis of this value and because of this value, man has the right to complete freedom of action. "Individualism and anti-individualism have to be utterly excluded because of their faulty interpretations and lack of understanding of the personalistic value of an act. . . . A self finds fulfillment only in a moral good; evil is always some sort of nonfulfillment."[70] The fundamental point is straightforward: Man has the freedom of action, the right to act, but does not have the right to do wrong. This determinism stems from law and corresponds simultaneously to the personalistic value structure.[71]

Applying Personalism

The purpose of this volume is to investigate the applicability of the insights of personalism to economics. Can personalist anthropology augment the work of economists in the modeling of human behavior and the study of human action? Our work now takes an economic turn. We seek a genuine synthesis of personalist theology and economics. In order to achieve this union of thought, we must now examine the discipline of economics, its history, anthropology, and modeling of human nature. Our thesis is that both theology and economics place the human person at the center of their analysis. The acting person is the basis of both personalist anthropology and economic analysis. By taking insights from both disciplines we hope to create a fuller, more useful anthropological basis for social science and economic personalism.

Notes

1. J. Patout Burns, ed., *Theological Anthropology* (Philadelphia: Fortress Press, 1981); Eugene Lauer and Joel Mecko, eds., *A Christian Understanding of the Human Person: Basic Readings* (New York: Paulist Press, 1982); and Wolfhart Pannenberg, *Anthropology in Theological Perspective*, trans. Matthew J. O'Connell (Philadelphia: Westminster Press, 1985).

2. John Paul II, "Analysis of the Biblical Account of Creation," in *The Theology of the Body: Human Love in the Divine Plan* (Boston: Pauline Books and Media, 1997), 27-29.

3. Emil Brunner, *Dogmatics*, vol. 2, *The Christian Doctrine of Creation and Redemption*, trans. Olive Wyon (Philadelphia: Westminster Press, 1952), 93.

4. Augustine, "On Original Sin," in *Augustine of Hippo: Selected Writings*, ed. and trans. Mary T. Clark (New York: Paulist Press, 1984). See also Jean Danielou, *Gospel Message and Hellenistic Culture*, ed. and trans. John Austin Baker (Philadelphia: Westminster Press, 1973); Jaroslav Pelikan, *The Emergence of the Catholic Tradition (100-600)*, vol. 1 (Chicago: University of Chicago Press, 1971).

5. Genesis 1:26 reads: "God said, 'Let us make man in our own image, in the likeness of ourselves.'"

6. Danielou, *Gospel Message and Hellenistic Culture*; and Pelikan, *The Emergence of the Catholic Tradition.*

7. Cf. David F. Ford, *The Modern Theologians: An Introduction to Christian Theology in the Twenieth Century*, 2d ed. (Cambridge, Mass.: Blackwell, 1997); and Philip Edgcumbe Hughes, *Creative Minds in Contemporary Theology: A Guidebook to the Principal Teachings of Karl Barth, G. C. Berkouwer, Emil Brunner, Rudolf Bultmann, Oscar Cullmann, James Denney, C. H. Dodd, Herman Dooyeweerd, P. T. Forsyth, Charles Gore, Reinhold Niebuhr, Pierre Teilhard de Chardin, and Paul Tillich* (Grand Rapids, Mich.: Wm. B. Eerdmans, 1966).

8. Brunner, *Christian Doctrine of Creation and Redemption*, 55-57.

9. Emil Brunner, *Man in Revolt: A Christian Anthropology*, trans. Olive Wyon (New York: Charles Scribner's Sons, 1939), 20-21.

10. Brunner, *Man in Revolt*, chapter 7.

11. Emil Brunner, *The Christian Understanding of Man* (London: Willett, Clark & Co., 1938), 159.

12. Brunner, *Man in Revolt*, 169.

13. Brunner, *Man in Revolt*, 114.

14. Brunner, *Man in Revolt*, 256.

15. Brunner, *Man in Revolt*, 258.

16. Brunner, *Man in Revolt*, chapter 11.

17. Brunner, *Man in Revolt*, 262.

18. Brunner, *Man in Revolt*, 262.

19. Brunner, *Man in Revolt*, 268-69.

20. Brunner, *Man in Revolt*, 270.

21. Brunner, *Man in Revolt*, 270.

22. Reinhold Niebuhr, *The Nature and Destiny of Man*, vol. 1 (New York: Charles Scribner's Sons, 1949), 3.

23. Niebuhr, *Nature and Destiny of Man*, vol. 1, 4.

24. Niebuhr, *Nature and Destiny of Man*, vol. 1, 16.

25. Niebuhr, *Nature and Destiny of Man*, vol. 1, 16.

26. Niebuhr, *Nature and Destiny of Man*, vol. 1, 16.

27. Niebuhr, *Nature and Destiny of Man*, vol. 1, 16, 170.

28. Niebuhr, *Nature and Destiny of Man*, vol. 1, 188.

29. Niebuhr, *Nature and Destiny of Man*, vol. 1, 199.

30. Niebuhr, *Nature and Destiny of Man*, vol. 1, 200.

31. Niebuhr, *Nature and Destiny of Man*, vol. 2, 251-52.

32. Niebuhr, *Nature and Destiny of Man*, vol. 2, 252.

33. See introduction to "Ressourcement: Retrieval and Renewal in Catholic Thought" series pages in Angelo Scola, *Hans Urs von Balthasar: A Theological Style* (Grand Rapids, Mich.: Wm. B. Eerdmans, 1995).

34. J. Ratzinger, foreword in Henri de Lubac, *Catholicism: Christ and the Common Destiny of Man*, trans. Lancelot C. Sheppard and Elizabeth Englund (San Francisco: Ignatius Press, 1988), 11.

35. Henri de Lubac, *The Drama of Atheist Humanism*, trans. Edith M. Riley (Cleveland: World Publishing, 1963), vii.

36. de Lubac, *Drama of Atheist Humanism*, 29.

37. de Lubac, *Drama of Atheist Humanism*, 31.

38. Gregory of Nyssa and Basil of Caesarea quoted by de Lubac, *Drama of Atheist Humanism*, 3-4.

39. Gregory of Nyssa and Basil of Caesarea quoted by de Lubac, *Drama of Atheist Humanism*, 5.

40. de Lubac, *Catholicism*, 29.

41. de Lubac, *Catholicism*, 33.

42. de Lubac, *Catholicism*, 34.

43. de Lubac, *Catholicism*, 39.

44. de Lubac, *Catholicism*, 33.

45. Karl Rahner, *Grace in Freedom*, trans. Hilda Graef (New York: Herder and Herder, 1969), 248.

46. Rahner, *Grace in Freedom*, 226.

47. Rahner, *Grace in Freedom*, 249.

48. Rahner, *Grace in Freedom*, 250.

49. Rahner, *Grace in Freedom*, 253.

50. Rahner, *Grace in Freedom*, 257-58.

51. Rahner, *Grace in Freedom*, 257.

52. Rahner, *Grace in Freedom*, 259.

53. Rahner, *Grace in Freedom*, 208-9.

54. Jacques Maritain, *Freedom in the Modern World*, trans. Richard O'Sullivan (New York: Gordian Press, 1971), 7.

55. The term *personalism* was first used by Schleiermacher in 1799, and then by Feuerbach in 1841, to characterize the position that God is a personal being, not an abstract principle. The poet Walt Whitman published an essay on personalism in 1868, and Bronson Alcott may have borrowed the term from Whitman.

56. Quoted by Rufus William Rauch Jr. in foreword to Emmanuel Mounier, *Personalism*, trans. Philip Mairet (Notre Dame: University of Notre Dame Press, 1952), xii-xiii.

57. Mounier, *Personalism*, xviii.

58. Mounier, *Personalism*, 3-5.

59. Max Scheler, *Formalism in Ethics and Non-Formal Ethics of Values: A New Attempt Toward the Foundation of an Ethical Personalism*, trans. Manfred S. Frings and Roger L. Funk (Evanston, Ill.: Northwestern University Press, 1973), 99.

60. Max Scheler, *On the Eternal in Man*, trans. Bernard Noble (London: SCM Press, 1960), 92.

61. Mounier, *Personalism*, 68.

62. These "tools" are mostly new ways of looking at epistemology. Intellectual intuition, or insight, is a central aspect of phenomenological realism. Phenomenology is a methodology for examining the human person that utilizes insights drawn from the essential features of human nature.

63. The work of Romano Guardini and Hans Urs von Balthasar also shaped Wojtyla's thought. Guardini elaborated the concept of "the world openness of the human person"—the ability of the human intellect not only to grasp but also to hunger for the eternal and absolute. Guardini made a detailed presentation of his views in the work *Person and World*, translated by Stella Lange (Chicago: Regnery, 1965).

Balthasar took aesthetic experience as his analytical starting point and outlined a theology and philosophy of human existence in his massive seven-volume work, *The Glory of the Lord: A Theological Aesthetics*, translated by Erasmo Leiva-Merikakis, edited by Joseph Fessio, S. J., and John Riches (San Francisco: Ignatius Press; New York: Crossroad, 1961-1969). He elaborates how faith is motivated by the Beauty of God, which is often described as God's glory. He details how genuine aesthetic experience can open the human soul to truth, goodness, and eventually the experience of the Divine. Balthasar understood the human person to be responsive to beauty. The beauty of the true, the good, and ultimately of God motivates persons in ways that mere intellectual argumentation cannot.

64. As quoted in George Huntston Williams, *The Mind of John Paul II: Origins of His Thought and Action* (New York: Seabury Press, 1981), 188-89.

65. Franz Böckle, ed., *Moral Problems and Christian Personalism* (Mahweh, N.J.: Paulist Press, 1965), 1-2.

66. Quoted in Williams, *The Mind of John Paul II*, 269-70.

67. Quoted in Williams, *The Mind of John Paul II*, 265.

68. Quoted in Williams, *The Mind of John Paul II*, 274.

69. Karol Wojtyla, *Toward a Philosophy of Praxis: An Anthology*, ed. Alfred Bloch and George T. Czuczka (New York: Crossroad, 1981), 25.

70. Wojtyla, *Toward a Philosophy of Praxis*, 41-42.

71. Wojtyla, *Toward a Philosophy of Praxis*, 42.

2

Economic Models of Human Nature

Economics As a Humanistic Discipline

Definition of Economics

Economics is considered to be the youngest of the social sciences. While economic writings date back as far as ancient Mesopotamia, it was through analyzing real economic inefficiencies in the late Middle Ages, as well as explanations of the Industrial Revolution that would follow, which helped economics to evolve into a coherent and distinct discipline. Until the beginning of the twentieth century, economics was considered to be one of the moral disciplines, that is, a discipline with a subject matter characterized by normative concerns relative to the natural sciences, yet distinct from the other social sciences in that positive applications also had relevance. If one wanted to learn political economy, one obtained a doctorate in moral philosophy. While positivistic tendencies grew in importance throughout the development of political economy, it was not until the acceptance of the Marshallian framework in this century that economics became predominantly positivist. Indeed, most of its history and tradition is firmly normative and concerned with moral issues.

Economics is an attempt to determine the best use of scarce resources to satisfy human wants. As such, economists are concerned with the study of the production, distribution, and consumption of goods and resources in society. To an economist, production refers to the creation of goods (and services); distribution, to the ways in which these goods are allocated; and consumption, to the ways in which these goods are used, either as final goods or as resource goods, which go into the creation of other final goods. Economic resources include not only gifts of nature, such as land, forests, or water, but also human resources, including human knowledge and labor. These goods and resources are directed in a world characterized by scarcity. Without scarcity, there would be no need for economics.

Economic analysis therefore studies the production, distribution, and consumption of any good or service given the constraint of scarcity. There are only so many trees available for the production of newsprint, only so much labor available for the production of hamburgers at your local McDonald's, and only so much time available for a mother to spend either at the workplace or with her children. How these goods are allocated involves choices, and the economist offers analyses of how these choices might be made. Positive economics provides value-free analysis, which finds those choices that promote economic efficiency; normative economics involves analysis based on promoting the values of a given society. In the United States, it is frequently the case that positive analysis finds the most economically efficient use of resources (that which results in the least waste), while normative analysis finds the most economically equitable uses of resources. The various schools of economic thought reflect the various biases inherent in our diverse society. Free-market schools, for instance, tend to maintain the view that government intervention in individual lives reduces human freedom, promotes economic inefficiency, and supports group interests over the common interest. Schools that tend to support government intervention in the economy deny that their policies impinge on human freedom and efficiency and, in fact, argue that their policies promote values such as equity and equality. Suffice it to say that it is the purpose of both positive and normative analysis to provide information about various economic choices available in given situations.

So far, the definition of economics offered is uncontroversial; it includes characteristics of the discipline that most economists would accept. Still, economics is notorious for producing varied definitions from its theorists. Lionel Robbins' definition is famous within the profession: "Economics is the science which studies human behaviour as a relationship between given ends and scarce means which have alternative uses."[1]

Background

There have been many prominent and influential economists who have shaped the discipline since the appearance of Adam Smith's *Wealth of Nations* in 1776. But for our purposes it would be more helpful to analyze some of the contributions made by those economists who have significantly influenced free-market economic thought in the neoclassical period. These are the economists who have written since the "marginalist revolution." This "revolution," occurring in the 1860s, refers to the insight that value is based not on, say, the amount of labor that is necessary to produce a given good, but instead on the value of the last unit of that good. This insight, discovered independently by Carl Menger, William Stanley Jevons, and Leon Walras within the same time frame, solved the diamond–water paradox,[2] which was the focus of much economic inquiry going back to the ancient Greeks. This theoretical breakthrough cleared the way for the modern neoclassical paradigm, which has dominated economic thought since Alfred Marshall. What follows, then, are very short biographies of some of the economists whose contributions laid the groundwork for the work being done by the free-market schools that are dominant today.

It is necessary to begin with the Austrian economist Carl Menger (1840-1921), whose books, primarily *Principles of Economics* and *An Investigation into the Method of the Social Sciences with Special Reference to Economics*, formed the foundation of other works that would eventually result in the Austrian School. Menger thought that the refinement of the theory of value was essential for solving all of the problems of economic theory that puzzled economists in his day. Explicitly, his analysis of the value of the unit of a good an individual would be most willing to part with signified the end to the labor theory of value, and the false predictions that derived from it. Implicitly, his methodology of providing a theoretical background for interesting historical work criticized the direction of both the classical school and the German historical school. Therefore, Menger occupied a unique intellectual position for his day. Allied with the British classical economists against the German historicists, he argued for a theoretical underpinning to the discipline of economics. But against these British economists, he argued first for the right theory, and second for the importance of its application. In the process, Menger established a firmer theoretical foundation for the study of the social sciences in general, while defending a subjective theory of value, which would become one of the defining tenets of the Austrian School.

Alfred Marshall (1842-1924) is best known today for taking the economic insights of classical English economists David Ricardo and J. S. Mill and incorporating them into a larger, coherent system of thought, which would become the bedrock of the neoclassical paradigm that dominates today.[3] Marshall's *Principles of Economics* is a landmark in the history of economic thought because it set forth an entire logical system of economics, made consistent with mathematical models and elegant graphs, which provided the basis for much of the scientific inquiry into economics that still occurs today. First published in 1890, it would teach generations of economists in its eight editions—John Maynard Keynes and Milton Friedman would later pay homage to Marshall's classic work. Marshall would prove to be the most influential economist of the twentieth century, and his *Principles* laid out the language by which economists communicate today. All schools of thought that gained credibility in the twentieth century—with the possible exception of the Austrians—did so on terms set forth by Marshall. His supply and demand theory, his presentation of Mill's joint supply system, and his explanation of *ceteris paribus*—the idea that we should analyze the effect of one variable on another, while holding all others constant—laid the foundation for the later work of J. R. Hicks, George Stigler, and Paul Samuelson. These economists would codify microeconomic analysis to the extent that today there is very little controversy about the basic principles of microeconomics.

Marshall thought economics was important because "the study of the causes of poverty is the study of the causes of the degradation of a large part of mankind."[4] Economic improvement comes about by examining institutions, incentives, and attitudes, investigation that required the spread of sound economic knowledge. This continuous examination and reexamination explains his Progressive Era motivation for constantly refining his famous text. Though not a statist, Marshall saw a redeeming role for government in the improvement of living conditions for the poor.

Ludwig von Mises (1881-1973) was an Austrian economist who built upon the work of Menger (and Menger's contemporaries) and in the process solidified what would become the Austrian school of economics. One of the most influential economists of the past century, his many books are still in print and widely read. His first major work, *The Theory of Money and Credit*, established Austrian monetary theory, showing the problems that can arise from currencies not backed by specie and in the control of a central banking authority. In the process, Mises integrated monetary theory into a microeconomic framework for the first time.

In 1920, Mises wrote *Socialism*, a book explaining why the basic tenets of socialism were not sustainable. Essentially, Mises showed how sound economic organization is impossible in the absence of market prices directing capital and labor to their most valued uses. Without market prices, it would be impossible for the socialist government to make the necessary economic calculations. This proved to be a prescient argument made during the height of the Progressive Era, when many economists extolled the possibilities of the public sector in bringing about a more efficient and just economy.

Mises's work seems the most relevant to the concept of economic personalism. He set forth the science of praxeology, a specific form of economic methodology that deduced economic laws from certain self-evident axioms, such as the fact that humans act. His magnum opus, *Human Action*, is his most comprehensive book in scope, as well as his most popular. In it, Mises integrates micro- and macroeconomic theory in a thorough, systematic manner, elucidating one of the most complete presentations of economic theory ever. At the same time, it presents a defense of classical liberal civil society.

John Maynard Keynes (1883-1946) is probably the most recognizable of any twentieth-century economist. To a large extent, the Keynesian framework has set the terms of the economic debates of this century. Keynes spent most of his professional life at Cambridge, where he became a household name early in his career as a result of his book *The Economic Consequences of the Peace*, which criticized the Allies' sanctions against Germany in the post–World War I years. Many considered Keynes's area of expertise to be monetary economics, and in the inter-war period he wrote three influential books that are still in print today, though mostly due to their historical interest. Of these, the *General Theory of Employment, Interest, and Money* would have the longest-lasting influence.

The *General Theory* provided an argument for an increased role for government in the face of economic downturns, essentially focusing on its ability to spur demand through the manipulation of interest rates. Though initially criticized by the mainstream economists of the day, the *General Theory* appealed to many of the younger economists who were not satisfied with the mainstream's explanations of the economic situation facing the world in the 1930s. One such economist, J. R. Hicks, took Keynes's framework and presented it in the form of a graphical analysis of the capital and labor markets, depicting the movement of both at different levels of interest rates. Hicks, who later won a Nobel prize in economics, recanted his belief in the legitimacy of the Keynesian system in the 1980s.

All Western governments adopted Keynesian fiscal policies in the years following World War II, and many economists credited Keynes with bringing the United States out of the Great Depression. Many economists besides Hicks studied Keynes and incorporated his framework into their own systems; many of these, including Milton Friedman and James Tobin, were awarded Nobel prizes in economics. In the late 1960s, Friedman remarked, "We are all Keynesians now," and Western governments implemented Keynesian policies of increasing government spending during economic busts, while decreasing it during booms. The problem is that governments found it easy to run deficits in order to spur economic growth, but eschewed the maintenance of surpluses during times of economic booms, giving in to a natural democratic inclination to spend more when possible. By the early 1970s, there were obvious discrepancies in the Keynesian system as increases in inflation (brought about by reductions in interest rates) did not bring about reductions in unemployment. The result—stagflation—caused Keynesian economics to lose credibility among many in the economic profession, and today most Keynesian economists refer to themselves as New Keynesians. These economists recast Keynesian principles to fit the realities of today's economy.

Friedrich von Hayek (1899-1992) was a prominent Austrian economist and, informally, a student of Mises who went on to have a career equally long and distinguished as his former teacher. In 1974, the year following Mises's death, Hayek received the Nobel prize in economics, adding much credibility not only to his work, but to that of the Austrian School, which at the time was beginning a revival that continues to the present.

In 1931, Hayek joined the faculty of the London School of Economics, where he developed a reputation in debates with Keynes and others concerning monetary, capital, and business cycle theories. A study of his debate with Keynes shows both an early rivalry followed by mutual respect, and the extent to which Austrian monetary analysis dominated the mainstream before Keynesianism took over in the following three decades.[5]

Hayek championed the principles of methodological individualism and subjectivism, coming to see their importance during his participation in debates on the possibility of sound economic policy in the absence of market prices. His short paper, "The Use of Knowledge in Society," is considered to be a classic.[6] In it, he explains that given the nature of knowledge—dispersed and under constant change—it is most effective when utilized by the people most affected by it. Because knowledge is dispersed throughout society, it is impossible for central planners to rationally direct the economy. Rather, entrepreneurs in the heart of the economy would be more likely to make the economically correct decisions. For Hayek, the difficulty of the central planner represents a coordination problem in socialist economies. However, much of Hayek's work focused on the reasons that coordination problems occur in market economies as well.

Hayek's work in this regard is based on the attempt to explain the reasons for economic depressions, phenomena that are accepted, but inadequately accounted for, in standard neoclassical analysis. According to Hayek, depressions result from a coordination failure within the economy—when goods are manufactured without a corresponding demand. Hayek identified this as *intertemporal discoordination*. Mainstream economics assumes instantaneous results from changes in economic variables; such results are easier to analyze and manipulate. But by introducing time into his analysis, Hayek was able to explain the reason for economic booms and busts, and he argued that there is no reason why economic growth should be marked by random upswings and downswings from an established growth pattern.

Hayek wrote *The Road to Serfdom* toward the end of World War II, warning of the propensity of unchecked government to grow at the expense of individual liberty. It was written for a more popular audience and probably ranks among the most read economic books of the twentieth century. It became both a best-seller and a book-of-the-month selection for *Reader's Digest*.

Milton Friedman (1912-) is perhaps the most influential living economist. Although there was already a Chicago School—defined by the work of Frank Knight, Thorstein Veblen, Henry Simons, Henry Schultz, and Jacob Viner—when he joined the faculty of the University of Chicago in 1946, Friedman embarked on a study of monetarism that eventually resulted in a new understanding of the role of money as well as of the Chicago School. By carrying on in the tradition of the great economists who preceded him, Friedman attracted some of the brightest minds to Chicago. This is evidenced by the fact that its Economics Department has the distinction of having the most Nobel prize winners on its faculty of any economics department in the country. Friedman himself was awarded the Nobel prize in 1976.

In the 1950s, Friedman formed the economic doctrine of monetarism, which is a modern explanation of the role that changes in the money supply has on price levels and economic activity. Friedman and his followers integrated the quantity theory of money—a macrotheory relating money supply to price levels—into neoclassical theory. Today, monetarism is associated with paying careful attention to monetary variables in the formation of government policy; it gained credibility in the 1970s when the Keynesian paradigm lost favor among economists.

Friedman's influence is also manifest in his research into permanent income, consumer theory, and the natural rate of unemployment. While his monetary theory constituted a major contribution to macroeconomics, Friedman also wrote a leading textbook on advanced microeconomic theory, *Price Theory*. Yet his influence is not limited to academic circles; his intellectual contributions have attracted mass appeal. His 1962 book, *Capitalism and Freedom*, written with his wife, Rose D. Friedman, became a best-seller. He began an economics column for *Newsweek* magazine in 1966, which he maintained consistently for almost twenty years. He has produced several television series on economics for public television, the most popular of which, *Free to Choose*, resulted in the best-selling book of that name. Friedman has also been active in politics, advising presidential candidates Barry Goldwater, Richard Nixon, and Ronald Reagan. His economic thought has shaped generations of economists, policymakers, and private citizens to an extent unparalleled since Keynes.

One of Friedman's contemporaries at Chicago, George Stigler (1911-1991), is another economist whose work influenced the economic policy of today. His research into the function of industry and governmental economic regulations won him the Nobel prize in 1982.[7] Stigler's initial studies of regulation compared prices of the same good in regulated and unregulated industries and found that regulation did not significantly affect prices. This research led to further studies into the unintended consequences of government regulations, and it added much empirical justification for the burgeoning Public Choice School.

Throughout his career, Stigler showed a concern for the protection of liberties in the face of governmental expansion in the Western democracies, a trait which partly defines the concerns of the Chicago School in the latter half of the twentieth century. But Stigler exemplified the Chicago approach in economic analysis by framing his arguments within an empirical and analytic framework.

Finally, the contributions of Gary S. Becker (1930-) are included in our list of significant moments in economics because Becker's analysis has broadened the scope of neoclassicalism to any area of life utilizing rational choice.[8] Becker, who also won the Nobel prize (1992), legitimized the inclusion of time in neoclassical models. Although the Austrians will rightly point out that they never excluded time from their systems, the neoclassical model has assumed instant market clearing in order to enable equilibrium analysis; for example, in order to assume that adjustments in, say, price and quantity will result in a definite, measurable level of output. Such results are more interesting to study; without them, the economist lacks clarity, and his or her analysis can devolve into nebulous conjecturing. By assuming instantaneous adjustment—among other neoclassical assumptions—economic tests offer definite results.

Much of Becker's work has been in the analysis of human capital. Capital theory assumes that it is in the producer's interest to improve his or her capital structure in order to increase output; Becker took neoclassical models of physical capital and applied it to humans. Just as the entrepreneur has an incentive to improve his or her production facilities, so does the individual have an incentive to improve his or her knowledge and skills in order to increase his or her income potential in the marketplace. Instead of investing in our existing capital structure, we also have an incentive to invest in ourselves to improve our earning potential. Following this reasoning, Becker found that more developed countries will tend toward higher levels of human capital relative to less developed countries. The individual with a very high earning potential will have a higher cost of time than the individual with a lower earning potential, and as a result, we would expect him or her to have a higher opportunity cost for nonincome-earning work in the household. Therefore, in advanced societies, in order to minimize higher time costs, we are more likely to see markets develop that cater to high-time-cost individuals. These people will eat out more, get their news from television as opposed to newspapers, be more likely to listen to music from CDs than at a concert, all because of their higher costs of time. The reinclusion of time into the dominant economic paradigm marks a major departure from the basic Marshallian structure, and it brings the views of the Chicago School closer to those of the Austrians.

Becker's human capital analysis also explains family size. To Becker, investment in children is similar to investment in consumer durable goods. He assumes that people choose to have children for future gain, both monetary and psychic. In societies characterized by lower incomes, the number of children is important to assure income in one's old age. This explains why we tend to see smaller families emerging in the industrialized West, where individuals tend to have higher earning potential, sound pension systems, and industries that are not tied to random shocks, such as agriculture.

Becker also greatly expanded on the study of economics as it pertained to the family unit. By applying his concept of human capital, Becker assumed that individuals maximize not only income, but also psychic "Z" goods. The level of

Z goods one maximizes is a function of income, but includes important and less measurable variables like the happiness one may feel from having a home-cooked meal or by taking one's child out to the mall. Becker's analysis then predicts that the single individual will choose marriage when he or she thinks that he or she can achieve a greater number of Z goods married than single. Becker goes on to apply this model to polygamous societies to predict the number of spouses an individual would choose, and to predict when individuals choose divorce. Hence, a marriage market results when examined in this fashion, in which people compete for the best mate.

In the 1960s, Becker instigated an advance in the economic analysis of crime. Prior to his research, economists assumed that the criminal's decision to commit a crime was based primarily on the likelihood of being caught and the severity of the punishment. Becker noted that by raising the cost of crime, society reduces the relative cost of committing more serious crime. Along this way of thinking, increasing the punishment for smuggling marijuana increases the incentive to smuggle cocaine, and increasing the punishment for smuggling cocaine in turn causes criminals to smuggle crack cocaine, and so on. By increasing the costs to the smuggler for dealing with both substances, society reduces the relative prices of each. Becker found that policies that increase the likelihood of being caught in general terms had the best chance of reducing crime. His analysis assumes that criminals are self-interested, rational individuals who weigh the cost and benefits of any purposeful action, an assumption that contradicted assumptions (which were once dominant) suggesting that the criminal mind was somehow degenerate.

Becker also tackled subjects such as the economics of discrimination, addiction, and democracy. Suffice it to say that he has legitimized the expansion of economic analysis beyond that which pertains to the common path established by micro- and macrotheory. His work certainly influences ours, because if it is indeed legitimate to establish the primacy of market forces in areas such as human fertility, then it is also legitimate to suggest the primacy of such forces in the study of the human person. His work shows that the market system, indeed any system involving trade in general, provides efficient solutions as well as new applications for policy, which are often not evident.

Free-Market Economics

The preceding thinkers, all of whom have contributed much toward the shaping of economics in this century, were dealing with a still evolving discipline, a system of thought that only recently would be considered a discipline in its own right (relative to the other disciplines). Each of the aforementioned economists considered himself a supporter of free markets. Each elaborated the conditions under which free markets could function in a free society, or they formulated policy that they thought would be necessary for the proper functioning of free markets. This sometimes implied differing concepts of the role of government in private market activity. For example, while Mises and Hayek thought a limited role for government was necessary for the health of free markets, both Keynes's belief in fiscal demand management and Friedman's support for a central bank policy targeting monetary aggregates imply support for the establishment of a larger governmental role. Keynes, for instance, believed that businessmen are governed by what he called *animal spirits*, that is, a tendency for businesses to act in unison. This meant that when they make decisions contrary to economic growth, it is not uncommon for them to do so in the aggregate, thus causing an economic recession. In pointing out what he then considered to be a negative result inherent in the market system, Keynes advocated a governmental role to encourage or discourage consumption through fiscal policy.

However, political economists have long marveled at the economy's tendency to function efficiently without the aid of a central planner. Whether it be Adam Smith's invisible hand, or Hayek's description of the use of knowledge in the economy, it was economists who first pointed out, and then attempted to explain, the fact that freer markets seem to provide the most efficient allocation of resources. This raises the question: What is a free market and how did it come about? The *free market* is defined as an economic market in which individuals are able to engage freely with others, to enter into contracts based on their own self-interest in which property rights are protected, and in which government involvement is kept at a minimum. It is characterized by entrepreneurs who risk their own wealth for the possibility of financial gain, based on the hope that their efforts will fulfill the needs and wants of consumers. In this system, the consumer has the final say as to whether the efforts of the entrepreneurs are rewarded. Given such a definition, it is obvious that such a system would evolve, and not come about as a result of central direction. As Hayek remarked in 1945, "I am convinced that if it were the result of deliberate human design, and if the people guided by the price changes understood that their decisions have significance far beyond their immediate aim, this mechanism would have been acclaimed as one of the greatest triumphs of the human mind."[9] The market system is mutually exclusive to command systems, and it was in arguing against the injustice and inefficiencies of the command system that a free-market economics was clarified.

This occurred in the late Middle Ages, at the height of the mercantilist system, when the major governments in the West were motivated to increase their countries' stock of specie. It was thought that a country's power, and therefore its security, lay in amassing supplies of gold and silver and in restricting the flow of these metals to other countries. This required the establishment of huge bureaucracies to manage many aspects of the economy. Each country's policies were geared toward exporting more of its produce than it imported, a goal that would be theoretically attainable only if a minority of the countries maintain such a policy, but not when all do so. The inherent inefficiencies of such a system became obvious. Huge corporations—each operating with the approval and aid of the state in the form of monopoly privileges, subsidies, and trade restrictions—grew very wealthy, at the expense of all other economic agents. When the Industrial Revolution was in its nascent stages, a middle class began to form in Europe that strongly opposed the continuation of this system. Even the leading mercantilist writers could not deny that their policies served the interests of the few at the expense of the many.

This was also the age of classical liberalism, when the idea that there is a natural law that supersedes laws of men was gaining acceptance among Enlightenment thinkers. It was out of this tradition that the Physiocrats, a group of thinkers in France, provided the most ardent support for free markets. These men argued that there was only a small number of natural laws, and that man-made law—which they called *positive law*—was legitimate only to the extent that it agreed with the natural law. The natural laws concerned individual rights of persons, including rights to property, and were knowable through human reason. A society that followed the natural law would contain only a few, necessary laws. This led the Physiocrats to fully develop and promote the doctrine of laissez-faire. In such a system, there would be little need for kings to govern; the natural law would govern. The belief that the lack of a central planner can result in the most economically efficient and beneficial results received its most strident support from the Physiocrats. They laid the intellectual foundation for free-market theory, which would later become the focus of economic study in Adam Smith's system and in economic analyses based on that system.

Their systems may seem extreme defenses for the free market, but they were developed in the face of some of the most extreme ruling government bureaucracies the world has ever known. They were never able to get their policy suggestions fully implemented by the ruling governments, but their ideas influenced the formation of the U.S. Constitution. Perhaps the closest the world has come to a free-market economy as envisioned by the Physiocratic writers can be found in the antebellum United States.

Free markets were the ideal among political economists in the nineteenth century, but toward the end of that century there was a strong movement to utilize the forces of government to further social goals. This was the Progressive Era, when the use of government intervention in the free market gained credibility among the intelligentsia. The Marshallian framework provided a mathematical certainty to economic methodology that did not exist previously. Economic analysis was ripe for the exploration of avenues through which government could influence the market economy. The result was a new emphasis on analyses that incorporated a governmental role, though generally with the ostensible goal of protecting free markets. However, policies that support governmental intervention and policies that are necessary for the successful functioning of the free market can be mutually exclusive depending on their formulation. When government intervenes in ways that force others to forego consumption to enable a redistribution of wealth, it does so at the expense of investment in the economy, causing individuals to favor consumption over investment. The result is not a zero-sum transfer; rather, it is the loss of benefits that would normally accrue under a regime of free markets. It is not surprising, then, that this century has seen the rise of free-market schools of thought that have developed largely in response to the economists' acceptance of the state in this century. Though different in significant ways, these schools of thought have endeavored to recapture aspects of the free-market economy and have incorporated the analytical tools of twentieth-century economics into their respective systems. In many ways they are complementary and overlap each other, while in other, more subtle ways, they differ in approach, definition, and methodology.

As mentioned earlier, the Chicago School has a history extending back to the beginning of the twentieth century. Since the 1920s, some of the most prominent economists ever to teach in the United States were based at Chicago. The seeds of the present school, however, can be traced to the influence in the department of Jacob Viner and Frank Knight. Both were on the faculty during the 1930s and 1940s, and both had enormous influence on the generation of economists that would follow. Though they had deep methodological differences, they did agree on the primacy of neoclassical price theory, and both opposed the new theoretical directions the discipline was taking in the 1930s, especially the theory of monopolistic competition and Keynesianism. This caused the department to develop an institutional opposition to New Deal policies in the 1930s and to Keynesian fiscal policies in the 1940s and 1950s. This differentiated it from many economics departments nationwide.

Today, the department is characterized by a belief in neoclassical price theory to explain economic behavior; a belief in the free market to allocate resources and income in the most fair and efficient manner; and a tendency to disregard the ability of governmental activity to improve upon market performance. By avoiding tempting intellectual fads of the past, it instead decided to focus on its comparative methodological advantage in neoclassical price theory and has been overwhelmingly successful. The Chicago School is now considered by many to be the most prominent economics program in the world. Its economists advise emerging governments on how to manage their economies along the Chicago monetarist model. By placing emphasis on the importance of empirical research, it has encouraged the application of positive methodology in all the social sciences. It has emerged as one of the primary proponents of free markets in the neoclassical tradition.

The Public Choice School, frequently referred to as the Virginia School because of the affiliation of many of its beginning adherents to universities in the state of Virginia, is usually said to have begun with the publication of *The Calculus of Consent* by James Buchanan and Gordon Tullock in 1962. While much proto–Public Choice literature existed prior to 1962, the Buchanan–Tullock book was the catalyst for further research that would form Public Choice analysis into a distinct school of thought. In 1969, the journal *Public Choice* began publication, and in 1986 Buchanan was awarded the Nobel prize for his role in creating and promulgating the study of Public Choice.

So, what is the Public Choice School? Prior to public choice research, political scientists' and economists' research into public-sector decision making assumed that public-sector bureaucrats were motivated by the public's interests. Individual theorists may not have believed this, but their theoretical model assumed benevolence on the part of public servants. The model was known as the public-interest model of public-sector behavior.

In the 1950s, however, when statistical techniques were first being utilized to test theory, it was found that the public-interest models did not stand up to empirical tests. Another theory, known as the interest group theory, began to gain credibility, in large part because it passed empirical testing. This theory simply extended the self-interest axiom to public-sector decision makers. Both public and private decision makers were considered to be utility-maximizing, but while non-public-sector decisions were assumed to maximize variables such as income or leisure, public-sector decision makers were assumed to maximize variables such as power, budgets, and prerequisites. By analyzing these other variables maximized in the public sector, public-choice theorists were able to develop models that had predictive power.

It is assumed in economics that businesses have an incentive to collect rents. This means that businesses will enter situations in which they can earn a greater-than-normal profit, a normal profit being one that pays all the factors of production and rewards the entrepreneur for risk taking. When the business earns a greater-than-normal profit, it is said to be collecting rents. When this occurs, there is an incentive for other businesses to enter the market. According to economic models, this will happen until every business in a given market is earning a normal profit. (When less-than-normal profits are being earned, businesses leave the market.) Economic theory supports the idea that no business can earn rents in the long run without the help of governmental intervention in the market, such as imposing regulations that increase the cost of market entry or restricting competition. The incentive to collect rents is the impetus for much business activity.

Since businesses have an incentive to collect rents, public choice theory has pointed out that it would be in a business's interest to "purchase" from the political market favors that enable it to collect rents. Without restrictions on government's ability to provide these favors, government impedes on free-market activity, causing market allocation to retreat from productive activity that increases our standard of living, toward activities that benefit a few well-placed public servants who are in a position to create rent-seeking opportunities for themselves.

The Public Choice School has been influenced by the Chicago economists; indeed, Buchanan earned his Ph.D. from Chicago under Frank Knight. As a result, it has emerged as the other strong proponent of free markets in the neoclassical tradition. It has been said that Public Choice is nothing more than political science analyzed with the tools of economic methodology. It added a credible analysis of the market process, suggesting that government activity can cause markets to fail. As such, it also complements the Austrian theory of the trade cycle from a positive, neoclassical point of view.

An Economic Understanding of Human Nature

Mathematical Modeling of Human Behavior

Mathematical modeling in the social sciences is by and large a twentieth-century phenomenon. While in economics there are exceptions to the rule—Sir William Petty's chimney counting in the late seventeenth century is a famous example—the ability to apply econometric techniques was aided by the introduction of the computer to empirical analysis. Most economists—even those who eschew mathematical applications in their research agendas—recognize a proper role for mathematical applications in the discipline. The debate among economists is over the extent of that role. Mathematical modeling certainly developed hand in hand with the development of neoclassical economics in the twentieth century.

A mathematical model can be simple or complex. The validity of a model in economics lays in its predictive power. If we define economics as the study of human action, then the assumption of the mathematical model is that by incorporating all of the variables that caused an action in the past we can construct a model with which we can predict how action might take place in the future. For example, economists assume that certain commodities have particular price elasticities. This refers to the change in demand that results from a change in the price. Certain goods, such as gasoline, electricity and other utilities, and cigarettes, have low levels of elasticity. The change in demand for these goods is relatively invariant to changes in prices. Other goods, such as Hershey candy bars, television sets, and Clorox bleach, have high levels of elasticity. The higher the elasticity, the more demand will change due to a change in price. So if the price of a Hershey candy bar were to triple, an economist would assume that less quantities of Hershey bars would be demanded; however, if the price of electricity were to triple, economists think that the demand for electricity would not change as much.

The mathematical model used to measure various elasticities would include variables that determine the demand for a given good. The variables for Hershey bars, one would assume, would include such factors as the price of Hershey bars, the price of other snacks, income, and age. All are measurable variables. By including these variables into a demand equation, economists can determine the elasticity of this good. By utilizing mathematical models in this manner, economists can make specific statements about human nature. For instance, if the price elasticity of demand for Hershey bars is -1.5, then economists would predict that a 10 percent increase in the price of Hershey bars would result in a 15 percent reduction in demand for them.

This is a relatively simple example of the role of mathematical economics. There are much more complex equations, but their validity lies in their predictive power. Mathematics is a language,[10] and it has validity in economics only to the extent that it correctly describes the theory. Economists prefer to state their theories in mathematical terms whenever possible. Randall G. Holcombe writes that the practice of restating economic theories in mathematical language, when possible, shows the inherent truth of the model.[11]

Mathematical economics is just another way of analyzing historical data. Data, after all, are measurements of events that have happened in the past, and since the validity of the model is based on its ability to predict, the implicit assumption of economic models is that future results are based on past results. While there is a limit to this assumption, it does provide relative assurance of the soundness of economic predictions in most cases. This assumption, however, is not based on economics but historical generalizations. It is important for the economist to distinguish between historical regularities and the theory when utilizing mathematical models. Otherwise, the same level of certainty is ascribed to the economic model that a natural scientist would ascribe to a model tested in a laboratory. It is important for the economist to remember the limits of his or her mathematics. Human behavior and the rationale for acting in a certain way varies from context to context. A test conducted in the social sciences may not yield the same results in every situation, in contrast to tests conducted in the natural sciences.

The Usefulness of the Models

Both the Chicago and the Virginia Schools utilize mathematical models in their systems; indeed, the use of mathematics has served to make their theories credible. As we have said, the application of mathematics to economics was one of the defining characteristics of the Chicago School, and the Virginia School can be partly seen as a derivative of Chicago economics. Certainly the failure of the public-interest theory to withstand mathematical tests, and the concomitant success of the interest group theory to pass such tests, served to give the Public

Choice School validity. (And just as certainly, the inability to test much Austrian theory, due to its basis in subjectivism, leads many in the academy to avoid its methodology.) Both schools of thought have been able to grow because of the adaptability of their systems to empirical testing. The majority of papers found in Chicago and Public Choice journals include results from the testing of mathematical models, leading one to believe that it is rare for a school of thought to develop in the absence of mathematical applications. The fact that the suppositions of both schools withstood mathematical testing was imperative for their respectability, credibility, and growth.

Philosophical Foundations and Sources

The philosophical foundations of the Chicago School can be traced to the decision on the part of that school to avoid the emerging "New Economics" in the 1930s. Since the New Economics supported a central role for the state, the Chicago economists were able to offer a contrary analysis to the reigning Keynesian framework. However, the Chicago School is not monolithic. It has been defined by the work of relatively few economists, so that their free-market reputation may have been developed due to its opposition to statist Keynesian models.

But when individuals refer to the Chicago School today, they usually have in mind the foundational work of Friedman and Stigler. Becker, who also writes in the tradition of the Chicago School, models his work on the neoclassical methodology championed by his predecessors. This school is characterized by the following strains of thought. First and foremost, it has championed neoclassical price theory, which refers to the use of partial equilibrium analysis of households and firms. Both Friedman and Stigler have written graduate-level texts on price theory—both entitled *Price Theory*—which are still widely used in graduate programs around the country. Friedman's article, "The Methodology of Positive Economics," is a classic in the social sciences. It would be on the short list of any economist's collection of the most read articles in economics. In this article, Friedman bolsters the assumptions necessary for neoclassical theory—and therefore for Chicago's price theory—to hold. Friedman argues that the truth of a model's assumptions is not as important as its predictive power; this statement enables the utilization of neoclassical theory in the face of its unrealistic assumptions, such as those made by the perfectly competitive model. Any argument that attacks the neoclassical framework as being unrealistic is then dealt with by emphasizing the model's ability to predict.

The Chicago School is also characterized by a general belief in the superiority of neoclassical monetary theory over Keynesian demand-side solutions. However, individual Chicago economists differ on the extent to which they part company with the Keynesian analysis. This even applies to Friedman, perhaps the school's most ardent anti-Keynesian, who wrote in 1968, "We all use the Keynesian language and apparatus; none of us any longer accepts the initial Keynesian conclusions."[12] This tendency again shows the influence of the Chicago economists of the 1930s in opposition to the Keynesian system. The primary difference between the Chicago monetarists and the Keynesians lies in their debate about the fluctuation of money in response to changes in interest rates. Chicago economists believe that money remains stable in response to changes in interest rates (i.e., it is not elastic with respect to changes in interest rates), while Keynesians hold that money is not stable in such cases.

The Chicago economists tend to believe that demand is elastic with respect to price, while most other schools believe that prices are inelastic. To use the Hershey bar example again, these economists would hold that a change in price would result in a larger change in demand than many other economists would predict. Again, this distinction is one of the important ways that Chicago economists differentiated themselves from the Keynesians, who hold that prices are "sticky," meaning that they do not adjust and that markets tend not to clear (in the short run). The idea of instant market clearing is essential for neoclassical, and therefore traditional, Chicago analyses.

Finally, Chicago-type analyses tend to accept the normative view that freedom is an important element in the economy. This may seem obvious given what has been written thus far about Chicago School theories, but aside from their opposition to Keynesian fiscal policy, there is nothing in their analysis that would necessitate laissez-faire. It is generally accepted by free-market neoclassical economists that there must sometimes be a trade-off between the goal of economic efficiency and other societal goals, such as maintaining the stability of a particular sector, promoting investment in particular industries, or maintaining cash transfers to specific public-sector interests (as in the case of school vouchers). In such a trade-off, Chicago economists tend to underscore freedom over other goals. While this emphasis may not be evident in the monetary policy of Chicago economists, it is notable in their analyses of welfare programs, government regulation, and drug and crime policies.

The Public Choice School can be viewed as a subset of the Chicago School. The important University of Chicago journals—*The Journal of Political Economy* and *The Journal of Law and Economics*—are filled with Public Choice analyses. While, the *Public Choice* journal (founded by Buchanan and Tullock) is characterized by Chicago-type empiricism. Public Choice theory assumes that businessmen maximize their private interest, not that of the public. Although they may engage in activities that support common public concerns—say, by supporting the local symphony or participating in the local chapter of the United Way—Public Choice theory assumes that their primary interest is in the advancement of their private business interests. Even their support of the public interest can be viewed as a way of advancing their private interest. So long as the attendant publicity or public goodwill generated by their investments in the advancement of the public interest results in net gains in profit, then public-sector investments can be justified on private grounds. They are viewed as acting so as to benefit themselves. This applies not only to Public Choice theory, but also to the greater body of traditional economic thought as well.

The important difference is in assigning this quality of self-interest to the public sector. Traditional economic analyses held that government officials promote the public interest before their private ones. The significant contribution of the Public Choice School was to assume that private interest also dominates governmental activity. It assumes that just as individuals in private-sector bureaucracies act in ways that will result in advancement within their companies, so too do public-sector bureaucrats have the incentive to produce policies that result in advancement within their bureaus.

Public Choice theory has extended this analysis to acquire an economic understanding of the voter. To the extent that economists analyzed voter activity, they assumed that he or she had sufficient incentive to be informed about the issues in a democracy. Public Choice theorists have developed the model of the rationally ignorant voter in which, given the time costs involved in becoming informed, especially in a complex society, there are many issues about which it would not be in the voter's economic interest to maintain knowledge. How many agricultural bills are considered in Congress having no effect on the business of the urban dweller? Given the cost of being informed about such bills, the rational city voter will choose to be ignorant of them. This tendency is compounded by the fact that the costs of these bills are socialized; the cost per voter would be very low. According to Public Choice theorists, politicians and bureau chiefs exploit this rational ignorance and maximize political contributions, votes, and power.

Public Choice theory has promoted the efficiency of free markets by analyzing the effects in the economy of rent dissipating behavior. This refers to the ability of businesses to garner special treatment by government. Assume that Company A could gain a million dollars a year in profit by obtaining special legislation. Economic theory would argue that it would be in the interest of A to spend up to a million dollars in order to get the special legislation. (In fact, studies show that companies will frequently spend in excess of the anticipated profit resulting from special treatment.) The money spent, however, is removed from the economy. It is paid directly to public-sector employees in the form of bribes, to lobbyists who will then promote this legislation, or to various elements of the media to promote governmental policies that might bring about the legislation. In the aggregate, this removes money from normal economic activity, reducing consumer choice, investments in labor, research and development, and, in fact, economic growth. Public Choice theory supports the implementation of a strong institutional framework to restrict the ability of individuals in both the public and private sectors from engaging in such activity.

Conclusion

In discussing the philosophical foundations of today's dominant free-market schools, we describe in more detail the assumptions about human nature made by each. This is not an easy task. The Chicago and Virginia Schools, as has been mentioned above, are comprised mostly of economic positivists. As such, their theory is validated by empirical evidence. Empirical data are important to bolster theory, but they are not always applicable to the study of human nature. The bias inherent in methodological positivism lies in disregarding theoretical constructs that are not susceptible to empirical research. It is rare for the Chicago and Virginia Schools to make assumptions about human nature that are not measurable; rather, they utilize data relevant to human nature, present models of that behavior, and predict how future behavior will be, given their analysis of the past.

This is not meant as an insult to this methodology. There is an important role for such methods of analysis in economics, not the least of which is the necessity of data to amass credibility for a school of thought. Indeed, if any new theory is formulated, and if it is amenable to empirical testing, one would want to see the results of this research to form opinions about the validity of the theory. For example, earlier we discussed the elasticity of a Hershey candy bar to demonstrate how an economist would interpret the results of a mathematical model. Assume that a confection industry economist analyzed market data and determined the elasticity of the Hershey bar to be -1.5. She may then make economic predictions about how human nature changes in response to changes in prices, but, in fact, she realizes that elasticity is a historical measure for a given time period within a specific culture. If the data collected were monthly data going back five years in South Carolina, then the computed measurement actually only describes the past market realities for Hershey bars in the last five years in South Carolina. So far, this has nothing to do with economic theory. It is actually a form of historical analysis. The economist should not read more into her findings beyond that it supports the Law of Demand, which would have been proven whether the elasticity test was conducted or not.

Another problem with the mathematical positivism championed by the Chicago and Virginia Schools is that in their reliance on differential calculus, they assume that human action takes place in finitely small, but discrete, steps. That is, after all, the domain of calculus. Whether this corresponds to actual, purposeful, human actions is doubtful, and this should raise doubts in the minds of those who rely on this tool of measurement. This highlights the point Friedman made in his essay on positive economics referenced above. The mathematically necessitated assumption that humans act in infinitely small measures is negated by the predictive power of the models that employ the assumption.

The overuse of mathematics is an attempt to make economic analysis utilize the same tools and enjoy the same certainty as the natural sciences. The term *mathemetosis* describes the tendency to use math when other forms of communication would suffice. In promoting the use of math in economic analysis beyond its proper role, these schools risk their own ability to speak to that which is not amenable to mathematical analysis. Although much of economic theory cannot be measured, these schools focus only on what can, thus leaving many areas untouched.

Yet both schools are, in fact, supportive of the free market. This has less to do with their methodology than with the realism of the assumptions made on the part of the great names associated with each. Many contemporary socialists, and indeed most New Keynesian economists, employ as much if not more positive methodologies in their analysis. The appeal of the Chicago and Virginia Schools lies not in the elegance of their models, but in the basis of their theories in truth.

Notes

1. Mark Blaug, *Great Economists since Keynes: An Introduction to the Lives and Works of One Hundred Modern Economists* (Totowa, N.J.: Barnes and Noble, 1985), 205.

2. This paradox describes the inability to explain why water, which is necessary for human life, is almost universally less expensive and seemingly of less value than diamonds, which are not. For more detailed information on this controversy, see Joseph A. Schumpeter, *History of Economic Analysis* (New York: Oxford University Press, 1954), 300-302; and Alejandro A. Chafuen, *Christians for Freedom: Late-Scholastic Economics* (San Francisco: Ignatius Press, 1986), 175.

3. Cf. Robert B. Ekelund Jr. and Robert F. Hebert, *A History of Economic Theory and Method* (New York: McGraw-Hill, 1975), 341-49.

4. Alfred Marshall, *Principles of Economics: An Introductory Volume*, 8th ed. (London: Macmillan, 1920), 3.

5. See John P. Cochran and Fred R. Glahe, *The Hayek-Keynes Debate: Lessons for Current Business Cycle Research* (Lewiston, N.Y.: Edwin Mellon Press, 1999), 68-94.

6. See Friedrich von Hayek, "The Use of Knowledge in Society," in *The Essence of Hayek*, ed. Chiaki Nishiyama and Kurt R. Leube (Stanford, Calif.: Hoover Institution Press, 1984).

7. See, for instance, George Stigler, *The Citizen and the State: Essays on Regulation* (Chicago: University of Chicago Press, 1975).

8. Becker's major works include *Human Capital: A Theoretical and Empirical Analysis, with Special Reference to Education* (New York: National Bureau of Economic Research, 1966); and *A Treatise on the Family* (Cambridge, Mass.: Harvard University Press, 1991).

9. Hayek, "Use of Knowledge," 122.

10. The phrase "Mathematics is a language" can be found on the title page of Paul A. Samuelson, *Foundations of Economic Analysis* (Cambridge, Mass.: Harvard University Press, 1947), which was the first major mathematical economics book. The phrase is attributed to J. Willard Gibbs.

11. See Randall G. Holcombe, *Economic Models and Methodology* (New York: Greenwood, 1989), 42-45. Holcombe notes, however, that not all economic theory can be stated in mathematical terms.

12. Milton Friedman, *Dollars and Deficits: Living with America's Economic Problems* (Englewood, N.J.: Prentice-Hall, 1968), 1-16.

3

Constructive Dialogue

Theological Reflections on Economics

To produce a synthesis of theology and economics is a fairly complicated project. It is not enough merely to lay side by side the outlines of each discipline. Such comparisons, contrasts, and attempts at intellectual union require focus and specificity. In this work, we are primarily concerned with a synthesis on the level of anthropology. Personalist theology offers one vision of the human person. Economics relies on an anthropological vision as well. Our efforts in the next few sections involve examining ways to increase the effectiveness of economics through the addition of insights from personalism. This section is the theologian's response to economic modeling. The following section provides the opportunity for economists to reply.

The Scope of Our Reflections

A theologian reading the chapter "Economic Models of Human Nature" must recognize the autonomy of economics as a discipline and the particularity of the methods appropriate to that discipline. In doing so, the theologian recognizes that, qua theologian, he or she has nothing to say regarding the adequacy of the methods and principles internal to the discipline of economics, including the way in which models of human nature are established and employed. Any critical remarks relative to the models of human nature employed must originate external to the discipline of economics and thus are not criticisms that question the *usefulness* of such models for the purposes of economists.

The understanding of the human person that emerges from theological reflection is far deeper and more complex than any economic model could possibly mirror or incorporate. This is to be expected, since economics as a discipline is concerned with a restricted realm of human activities and with such phenomena as prices, money, the supply and demand for goods and services, and market structures and processes. Models of the person in this context have an essentially instrumental character and are restricted by the limited purposes of economists. In contrast, theological reflection is not concerned with creating models of human nature that have predictive power; in fact, it is not concerned with models in the strict sense of the term. Drawing from revelation and from human experience, theology is concerned with attaining a deep understanding of the human person, both his or her nature and his or her condition, and in particular, his or her nature and condition relative to God. Economics has little to offer such reflection, and it would be unrealistic and unwarranted for a theologian to demand or expect economics to either contribute to a theological understanding of the person, or for economics (as a discipline) to incorporate explicitly theological notions or principles.

What is the purpose, then, in bringing theological anthropology and economics into dialogue? What is the sphere of overlap between the two disciplines that would constitute a common concern (even if that sphere were approached by theology and economics in two fundamentally different ways)? The answer is relatively straightforward. To the extent that economics is concerned with the human person and with human activity, it shares this concern with theology. This is true even when it is the case that the human person and human activity are examined according to different methods and are evaluated according to different principles and end within the respective disciplines. This is simply to repeat that the theologian qua theologian lacks the competence to judge the effectiveness or ineffectiveness of economic approaches and principles for the discipline of economics itself, and it is certainly not our purpose to judge ecnomics according to the principles that regulate theology. Nonetheless, when the theologian considers the human situation, he or she must concern him- or herself with all the activities of human life, and this necessarily includes economic activities. In what follows, we present some of the concerns that a theologian would bring to the consideration of these activities, as well as some of the reservations a theologian might raise relative to the assumptions about the human person in economic theory in general.

A Personalist Perspective

From a personalist perspective, a theologian can simply applaud any movement within economics toward an emphasis on human agency in understanding economic causality. The discipline of economics will become more humanized and more personalized the more it recognizes the centrality of the acting person. More specifically, it must recognize the centrality of *persons acting in cooperation* in its understanding and analysis of economic activities and events. In contrast, economic approaches that give primacy to abstract, nonpersonal forces (e.g., money supply, business cycles, depressions, and so on) tend to become dehumanizing and depersonalizing, since they focus on nonpersonal data, and, more important, tend to subordinate persons to nonpersonal forces and events. Furthermore, it would appear, an economics that relied too heavily on such nonpersonal data for all its analysis would be less accurate in its predictive power than a personalist approach. Of course, economics must also be concerned with all sorts of nonpersonal factors and causes. The question is one of emphasis and priority. If we lose sight of the fact that economics is a *humanistic* discipline, we will inevitably fall into all sorts of distortions concerning the nature of the acting person. These distortions should, at least formally, also lead to an inferior economics qua economics.

There are two specific concerns that the theologian would want to present to the economist. The first focuses on the activities and interactions among persons within the market, where the market is understood to be that sphere of activities concerned with producing, distributing, and consuming goods and services. The second focuses on the place and importance of market activities relative to other spheres of human life.

The Concern for Community

Nearly all twentieth-century social science, economics included, has a tendency to focus its analysis on individual human behavior. From a theological approach, this is more than acceptable. In a strictly philosophical sense, and from the perspective of social science methodology, analyzing collective behavior is nearly impossible. Our scope, if we desire accuracy and coherence, must be limited to explaining and predicting the behavior of the individual. Extrapolation then permits this initial data to be used for broader study and even predictions. Therefore, the theologian is not as concerned with methodological individualism as much as with an atomistic individualism that could result.

Atomistic individualism would be a secondary phenomenon that could occur from a valid use of methodological individualism. It is completely legitimate to isolate the individual person as an abstract singular reality for the sake of accurate and useful social science. It is, however, quite another matter to allow that initial predisposition of analysis to spill over into a quasi-moral or social theory. Methodological individualism, despite all its benefits, has the tendency to tempt its practitioners into a utilitarian and amoral social analysis that goes beyond what is required for proper economic analysis.

For example, self-interest is an anthropological presupposition common to many economic models. Methodological individualism would require that economists create their models from the perspective of the self-interested, utility-maximizing individual. Yet, the reality of the situation is that people rarely entertain cost-benefit analysis from the perspective of strict self-interest without regard for the interests and concerns of others. Most heads of households have to balance a wide array of interests: their own, their spouse's, their children's, their coworkers', and so on. Entertaining a reductionism in the name of methodological efficiency is acceptable. Allowing that reductionism to spill over to influence actual anthropological, social, and moral views, however, is not acceptable. What we are saying, therefore, is that it is fine to practice methodological individualism as long as one does not hold to an individualistic social philosophy that denies the reality of the social nature of the person.

The denial of the social nature of the human person eventually leads to the denial of the moral implications of market activity. Individualism can lead to an amoral approach to economic analysis, where the economist sets aside, unnecessarily, the role of moral values from his or her analysis. The theologian would be concerned with the various moral and morally relevant dimensions of the activities that delineate the market. For wherever persons interact with one another, moral questions arise and moral considerations are in play. Broad questions of justice, that is, fairness, honesty, and responsibility, are immediately relevant to such personal interactions. To put the moral question in general terms, we could ask how, in the competitive sphere of the market, do the demands of justice interface with the demands of efficiency and profit maximization? For while growth and efficiency are of central importance for economic activity *qua economic*, other considerations must enter in as long as persons are involved.

In a personalist framework, the question is not only one of justice. Based on the personalist principle that the human person is to be affirmed for his or her own sake, we can pose the central personalist challenge in the following way: Are the persons involved (e.g., employees, customers) viewed *merely* as means to the ends of growth and increased profits? It is important to note that the personalist principle forbids treating persons merely as means. Thus, it does not forbid treating persons as means in some sense, so long as they are not treated exclusively as such. This point is significant, since it is unavoidable that persons be seen as means to ends within the sphere of market activity; for example, an employee is necessarily a means to the end of production and a consumer is necessarily a means to the end of profit maximization. The personalist challenge is to constantly evaluate the ways in which persons are used as means in market activity. For example, the question of *who* is involved in the production and distribution of products leads to questions of fair pay and adequate working conditions. Further questions include concern for the effects of the production and distribution of products. These include effects on the environment and on the communities in which the products are manufactured and consumed. The theological and personalist concern here is not to replace the principles that govern market activity with the theological principles of justice and charity, but rather to insist that no sphere of human activity falls outside considerations of justice and charity. Moreover, it is to insist that market institutions recognize the primacy of the person relative to other nonpersonal goals and purposes.

The Concern for the Limitation of the Market

The second concern of the theologian actually consists of two parts. The first refers to the relative place and importance of market activities (working, producing wealth, buying, and consuming goods) within the broader context of personal, social, and cultural life. The second aspect involves the limits of economic analysis due to the fact that there are certain spheres of human activity not properly subject to cost-benefit analysis of the type performed in economics.

The human person is not only *homo economicus* (a wage worker and a buyer and consumer of goods and services); he or she is also a person bound to other persons in relations of responsibility, love, and caring. These are relations with others that are not constituted and regulated by or evaluated through cost-benefit analysis and the principle of efficiency. In other words, these relations are essentially different from market relations and operate according to their own principles. The human person is a being who desires to know and delights in knowledge for its own sake. He or she is a being who suffers—through his or her own failures and evil actions and through the evil actions of others—and who must face death. He or she is a person who seeks God and who is called by God. He or she is a person who is open to love that appeals beyond intellectual concerns of cost to self and disposes one to give oneself away to the beloved in acts of self-donation.

All of these dimensions of human life and activity fall outside the sphere of the market and cannot be adequately analyzed in terms of economic principles. This does not mean that they could not be subject to economic analysis in principle. Rather, it means that the nature of these relations and activities, as well as the principles that govern them, cannot be captured by economic analysis. Any attempt to do so would necessarily be partial and extrinsic. That is, since economics according to its own methods and principles cannot adequately determine the nature of these relations and activities, an application of economic analysis to them cannot address their inner nature, but only certain external dimensions of them.

Although most mainstream economists would agree with the above insights, there is a growing tendency toward economic imperialism—that is, a growing desire on the part of all social scientists to use economic analysis to explain such human realities as family life, love and marriage, education and moral training of children, and charitable activity. Perhaps the clearest examples of this economic imperialism can be found in the work of the Chicago School's Gary Becker on family life and marriage, and in Richard Posner's attempt at economic analysis of sex and romance. Stated simply, there are human realities that transcend the scope of economics, both in terms of the inability to place a price tag on many human goods and services, and of the inappropriateness of the attempt.

But it might be objected that economics is concerned with any and all choices of allocation of goods and determination of means in contexts of scarcity. By this definition, all human activity is economic, and therefore the study of such activity entails the economic method. But surely this definition is too broad and vague. As a social science, economics must be distinguished from, for example, psychology, sociology, cultural anthropology, political science, and comparative religion. This delineation among the social sciences is admittedly becoming blurred as other disciplines adopt the methodology of economics. In this way economics has proven itself and its models highly effective.

In a different way, however, economics must be distinguished from the methods and principles of philosophy and theology. In delimiting economics as a distinct discipline, one must ask the question: In what way is an economic analysis of activity distinctively economic? How is it distinct from a political analysis, a psychological analysis, or a specifically philosophical analysis? If the definition of economics is too broad, it becomes almost useless and allows the discipline of economics to claim competency in spheres of human activity where it simply does not belong. Just as some political scientists tend to analyze all human activity in terms of power, so an economic theorist might tend to view all of human activity in terms of cost-benefit analysis and judge it according to efficiency. In fact, human activity is far more complex than this framework allows.

For example, economics assumes a relatively simple theory of human motivation; something along the lines of a principle of maximization of goods, where a good might not only be a physical good, but also a psychic one.[1] The principle could be formulated this way: John chooses *x* over *y*, and *x* tends to maximize the goods A, B, and C to a greater degree than *y*, so John chooses *x* over *y* because *x* maximizes the goods A, B, and C. This understanding of motivation may be sufficient for the purpose of economic analysis, but it simply fails to account for many other forms of motivation. This failure can already be indicated when one considers the formal character of the assertion: from the fact that (1) the choice of *x* results in a greater maximization of goods than the choice of *y*, and since

(2) John chooses *x*, one cannot infer that 1 is the exclusive, primary, or necessary reason or motive for 2. The first reason is not exclusive, because there could be other motives; it is not primary, because there could be higher or deeper motives, and it is not necessary, because John could choose *x* without the motive of maximizing goods.

To dispute this last claim, one needs to make a claim about the general nature of human motivation. One could claim, for example, that human nature is such that rational human beings choose according to the principle of the maximization of goods. This is a strong, normative claim about human nature. As such, it is a philosophical claim that would have to be argued for on philosophical (and, therefore, extra-economic) grounds. In other words, this is not an economic claim supported by economic argument, but rather a philosophical claim that requires philosophical models, insight, evidence, and argumentation. Therefore, it poses a problem for anyone who conceives of economics as a positive, value-free discipline, since it requires a normative, philosophical claim as a basic principle of economic analysis.

It is probably safe to assume that most economists would not want to make strong, normative claims about human nature and thus go outside of economics to validate a central explanatory principle. Instead of claiming philosophical insight into the nature of the person, the economist could posit the principle of the maximization of goods as a hypothesis. Then, through extensive empirical investigations, he or she might determine whether, in general, when individual agents choose *x* over *y*, they do so because they think that the choice of *x* will maximize the goods A, B, and C to a greater degree than the choice of *y*. But here, too, a problem arises. In this case, the economist must assume the methods and results of empirical psychology, once again going outside of his or her discipline to establish a fundamental principle.

Presumably, as an economist, one only needs to establish the maximization of goods as a general principle with predictive power. Clearly, when an economist posits a principle such as the maximization of goods, he or she does not claim or mean to investigate what people actually *think* when they choose *x* over *y*. He or she merely wants to establish that the principle of the maximization of goods adequately explains human behavior and that this can be verified externally, that is, by examining how people actually behave and by analyzing that behavior in terms of the principle. Such an analysis may well be adequate to the goals of economics, but at the same time, it indicates the restricted character of the discipline itself. One could even say that an economist such as Gary Becker is not concerned with human action as such, but only human behavior since he needs only to determine a principle according to which certain cause–effect relations can be predicted.

The theologian is not only concerned with recognizing spheres of human life and activity that fall outside the competence of the discipline of economics.

He or she must also recognize the relative importance of market activity within human life understood more broadly. Any assertion about the importance or significance of market activity relative to other spheres of activity is essentially a value judgment. Making such a judgment might seem bold, but theology itself does not assume a value-free methodology. Rather, it assumes an objective hierarchy of values according to which different types of human relations and human activities can be assessed and judged. According to such an analysis, what we are here calling market activity must be seen as subordinate to activities that comprise social and political life (marriage and family, cooperation with others in the building and sustaining of community), activities that comprise religious life (seeking God, responding to God, worshiping God), and activities that comprise seeking after values, not simply to be consumed, but for their own sake (values such as knowledge for its own sake, music and art, friendship, and accomplishments as ends in themselves).

In claiming that the importance of market activity is subordinate to other spheres of activity, we do not mean to deny its absolutely essential character as an aspect of human life. Indeed, economic activity is inherently implied in each of the above and required for each of the above activities to succeed. What we are broadly calling market activity comprises all sorts of activities that are in and of themselves meaningful and have value for persons. Moreover, such activity is often the necessary condition for other sorts of activities that fall outside the sphere of the market. Nonetheless, the importance of such activities must be relativized. They are necessary to human life and often entail real meaning and value for the persons who engage in them. But the sphere of the market is not comprehensive, and the principles that govern such activities (efficiency, the weighing of costs and benefits) cannot be extended to other dimensions of human life without distorting and damaging those dimensions.

The theologian is thus concerned with safeguarding spheres of human activity and human life from being subject to economic analysis where the latter means analysis in terms of cost, benefit, and efficiency, and with safeguarding and promoting values that are not determined by market forces. This is particularly important in cultures such as our own where market activities are given priority in terms of value and significance, and activities falling outside this sphere tend to become devalued. Activities such as caring for and spending time with those we love (family life and friendship), artistic activities that endeavor to create something because it is beautiful and good, activities with others where the purpose is essentially social, and religious activities are often devalued in our culture simply because they do not easily lend themselves to economic evaluation. The absolutizing of market activity, that is, the assumption that market activities are the most meaningful and significant, not only leads to the devaluation of nonmarket activities; it also tends toward the devaluation of persons who do not engage in the market. There are, for example, persons who cannot produce—children, the elderly, handicapped, and sick—and persons who choose not to produce—for example, parents who stay at home and care for their children, and artists who choose to devote themselves to their art. There are also persons who do not consume sufficiently (the poor), and these two groups (those who cannot produce and those who do not consume sufficiently) very often coincide.

In a culture such as our own, the theologian's role is essentially prophetic. He or she has the task of reminding us that the person is not only a worker and a consumer, but also a member of various communities (e.g., family, church, neighborhood, organizations, nation), a bearer of responsibilities, obligations, and rights, worthy of a certain degree of respect, and ultimately responsible before God.

Conclusion

It is important that our criticisms be taken in context. This work is seeking a synthesis of economics and theology, not a dispute over methodology and the scope of economics. Yet, to achieve our synthesis we must also engage in critical evaluation. For only through constructive and honest dialogue can the two disciplines hope to learn from one another.

We must conclude this section by recognizing the fact that merely stating theological truths and profound anthropological insights is not enough to achieve our goal. To criticize the economist for being reductionistic, imperialistic, or lacking sophistication is ultimately unhelpful if it does not lead to attempts to make such criticism useful to the economist. Most economists will reply to our criticisms, and rightly so, by insisting that their discipline works. Perhaps economists work from philosophically or theologically faulty models, yet these models still maintain predictive power and practical usefulness.

The theologian's task is to convince the economist to take his or her anthropological insights seriously enough to integrate them into the discipline. Theological insight will only prove interesting and helpful to economists when it can be demonstrated to lead to better economic analysis. For this task we must rely on the expertise of the economists themselves. Most theologians do not possess the ability to create real, useful economic models or to alter adequately the model's presuppositions. Economists must be convinced to enter into meaningful dialogue with theologians so as to be able to take such criticism, offered in good faith, back to their own disciplines. Our next section is just such an attempt.

Economic Reflections on Theological Anthropology

There are a number of reasons a serious consideration of personalism from the perspective of economic methodology has not yet been attempted. But the primary one has more to do with the incentive structure of graduate economic education than with the lack of interest in a viable synthesis of these two fields of study. Graduate economic students are encouraged to develop two or more areas of specialization in the course of earning their doctorates, and once they begin teaching assignments at universities, reward structures generally encourage the continued publication of research articles within those areas. Accreditation programs and funding are often tied to the number of articles placed in refereed journals. The referee process encourages articles resulting from a predetermined set of classifications within economics. Research conducted outside of this predetermined set is less likely to be published and therefore less likely to be undertaken. It is not within an economist's best interest to devote time to new areas that offer little immediate professional recognition. As a result, research focusing on synthesizing economic methodology and personalist thought has not yet piqued the interest of professional economists.[2]

Yet, analyzing various ways in which personalist ideas are congruent with economic methodologies is important if doing so provides a better understanding of the source of any economic action, namely, the acting person. To the extent that the study of personalism accomplishes this task, economic interest in personalism will increase. The areas of agreement between the two disciplines are not immediately apparent to many economists. Concepts such as human dignity and Christian anthropology do not fit into the modern neoclassical framework within which most economists communicate today. In this section, we present some similarities and differences between personalism and economics, and some possible applications of an economic personalism. We hope to demonstrate that an economic personalism can be developed within the framework of accepted economic methodologies and that the study of economic personalism provides a more realistic presentation of the person than that utilized by most schools of economic thought.

Similarities

The study of personalism throughout the twentieth century represents an effort to understand the human person as he presents himself in the world, and not as various philosophical models present the person. In social science methodology, practitioners often develop methods that assume characteristics about the human person that are not entirely accurate. Marxists, for instance, never foresaw the ability of social institutions to adjust or compromise in the process of market economic development. Existential philosophers never fully respected the natural propensity in humankind to search for something greater than the individual. Such methodologies tend to be short-lived; they were developed to explain social phenomena more adequately than existing schools of thought. Personalism was developed by individuals who were troubled by the inability of established schools of thought within philosophy and theology to explain social crises that characterized much of Western civilization in the 1930s. Instead of proposing a logical system and assuming attributes of the human person that would support the coherence of the system, personalists started with the human person. They decided that systems that may develop should start from an accurate understanding of who the human person *is*.

Many advances in economic theory have been the result of employing a more realistic picture of human nature. For example, the market system was in part an outgrowth of correcting false assumptions about the importance of the human person made by mercantilist thinkers. The dignity of the human person or the role of the individual consumer in the economy was of secondary importance to the primacy of the king or the maintenance of gold flows into the country. Economies suffered as a result, and the success of the Industrial Revolution can be attributed to a more realistic assumption about the role of the individual. Firms that serve the needs of society best would be those that serve the needs of the individual rather than the government. When the demands of individuals change, firms would respond or go out of business. Actions of free individuals would dictate the size and scope of the economy.

Throughout the history of free-market economics, the uniqueness and dignity of the individual human person are paramount. The importance of the human person for economic activity explains much of the economic development in the West.[3] Beyond a certain point—of which it is beyond the scope of this book to identify—the growth of government inhibits freedom and interaction among individuals and becomes an impediment to economic development, as well as human dignity. The market system, like personalism, respects human freedom and dignity. In this system, entrepreneurs take an active interest in a correct anthropology of the human person, albeit for different reasons than do personalists. A richer understanding of persons is beneficial to the understanding of markets. Entrepreneurial action that serves the needs of individuals is rewarded, and entrepreneurs who possess an accurate understanding of the human person are best able to serve their needs. Businesses that no longer serve these needs remain afloat only to the extent that they are subsidized.

This similarity is strengthened by the fact that many personalists, especially those influenced by French thought, were troubled by the pernicious effects the large state would have on the flourishing of the human person. This concern was most clearly expressed by Emmanuel Mounier, who observed that the growing influences of nationalism, Communism, and socialism tended to inhibit the free actions of individuals. If one of the defining characteristics of the free human person is found in his or her ability to act, then social systems that restrict this ability also threaten to impede the development of fully human persons. Economic analysis likewise addresses the effect of a large state on the economy. Though the degree of acceptance of the proper role of the state in the economy differs among economists, free-market schools recognize a general deleterious effect on commercial activity resulting from big government. From this perspective, the personalist and the free-market economist share the same concern for the size of the state.

Personalism in this century represents an effort to reassert the primacy of the person in the philosophical realm. It affirms the free and creative nature of persons. The market system implicitly affirms these qualities by rewarding unrestrained actions that result from creativity with the aim of serving the needs and wants of others. Free-market schools in economic thought recognize the free and creative nature of the individual human person as something that can be capitalized on in order to promote economic growth and efficiency. Furthermore, any model employed or policy advocated by these schools does not make assumptions about what the human person *should be*, but instead bases its models on the perception of how the human person is. If the models do not seem to explain the economy realistically, then it is assumed that the perception of the human person is faulty, not that the result is from shortcomings in human nature per se.

The tendency to blame perceived shortcomings in human nature can be found in those schools of thought that do not affirm the freedom and creativity of the individual consumer or producer. To Keynes, the cause of economic depressions was the tendency of producers to act in the aggregate, undersupplying consumers in the process. The result was that those making better business decisions could not balance out the poor ones made by others. Keynes took the problem to be a shortcoming in human nature, which needed correction by fiscal policy. Free-market schools, on the other hand, are less likely to blame the individual human actors. These schools generally accept the idea that economic progress follows a steady pattern of growth, and that it is the tendency of governmental agents to intervene in economic activity that creates the phenomenon of economic booms and busts. They reject the idea that a psychological herd mentality must cause cyclical changes in the economy.

The Laffer Curve is an example of a free-market model that recognizes the primacy of individuals in the economy.[4] This model, first developed in the 1970s by economist Arthur Laffer, found that increases in marginal tax rates would only increase tax revenues up to a point, beyond which increases in tax rates reduce tax revenues. By arguing that lowering tax rates could actually increase tax revenues, Laffer integrated into his model the propensity for individuals to engage in economic activity within the framework of a tax system that recognized and rewarded their creativity in providing goods and services that are demanded within the market system. Furthermore, the increase in economic activity resulting from decreases in tax rates would not be the product of either a coercive state forcing the actions of individuals, or a large central government imposing an incentive structure designed to bring about predetermined economic and social results. Such free-market analyses respect human dignity. They are marked by a desire to take as their starting point the human person as he presents himself in the world in which he lives; they recognize that failed policies fail because they do not begin with an accurate representation of the human person.

Personalism's belief in humankind's a priori ability to recognize moral values is familiar to some economic methodologies. Much economic theorizing done today is based on belief in certain a priori truths. For instance, Ludwig von Mises's system of praxeology is based on certain a priori truths.[5] A primary belief among the Late Scholastic thinkers, which was maintained by eighteenth-century Physiocratic thought, by the nineteenth-century French economic tradition, and by some twentieth-century Austrian economists, is that natural-law theories form the basis for all economic conjecture. Not only is the belief in a priorism familiar to economic methodology, it has an accepted place within economic theorizing.

Personalism's concern for the marginalization of human beings in the face of rapid technological change is also similar to the Austrian critique of the neo-classical tendency to reduce humans to simply another element in the economic model, so that he or she is just another economic variable. Doing so reduces a human being to merely a means in economic life, as opposed to the end. Austrian analysis reasserts the primacy of the acting individual in defining economic activity and is critical of economic analysis that reverses this priority.

Finally, personalism recognizes the importance of belief in an afterlife for influencing human action. Moral theology defines freedom as the ability to choose to do the good so that we can be brought closer to God. When we do this, we are, in effect, choosing to accept or reject the rewards gained from Christ's sacrifice. There is an economic application of this tenet as well. There have recently been numerous studies on the effect of millennialism in economic life. Premillennialists hold that Jesus is returning soon, and that we may even be able to predict when this will occur by juxtaposing events in the headlines with biblical prophecies. This removes the urgency associated with much of economic organization. Postmillennialists, on the other hand, believe that Christ's Second Coming is something that will occur in the distant future, and that to prepare for it and hasten its occurrence, a Christian theocracy must be established. This mindset motivated many Progressive Era thinkers to support an active role for the state to bring about these societal changes to create the necessary utopia to which Jesus would return.[6] The traditional teaching on the millennium is amillennialism. It teaches that we cannot know when Christ will return, so excessive concern with God's timing is unnecessary except with respect to the preparation of our hearts. Societal positions on the millennium have a significant effect on economic activity. Personalism's recognition of the importance of the afterlife affects the way the human person chooses to act. The human person is motivated to live well now because all acts are committed *coram Deo* (before the face of God). This implies an incentive for the formation of safe, moral communities, support for a just economy, a commitment to helping the poor, and concern for those alienated by society. That all of these concerns influence the formation of economic life is significant; it implies that the idea of an afterlife affects how we treat each other.

Differences

While neoclassical analysis makes important assumptions about the human person, this school of thought is interested principally in the predictive power of its models. Given this goal, a neoclassically trained economist would have less professional interest in the study of personalism (although he or she might have interest for other reasons). Personalist rhetoric and ideas would not fit into this type of analysis. However, economists who consider themselves methodological subjectivists would be more likely to incorporate personalism into their analysis. Personalism also recognizes that there are areas of human nature that elude philosophical analysis. That is, personalists themselves acknowledge the utter complexity of the human person. When philosophers attempt to address these areas, they do so acknowledging the imperfections inherent in their approach. Economists—primarily those who are not methodological subjectivists—tend to avoid issues that do not fit into the logical framework of their models. This is usually tolerated as long as their models maintain predictive power. This explains the faddish nature of many economic models in which schools of thought tend to experience chimerical influence.

In contrast, Austrian economists avoid reductionism of this sort by avoiding analyses that reduce economic questions to relationships among a few, easily regressed variables. As a result, the personalist requirement to consider all the facets of the human person should be a smaller hurdle for Austrian methodology to negotiate than for their neoclassical counterparts. In fact, to the Austrian, thicker descriptions of the actions of persons clarify economic phenomena better. In a neoclassical analysis, engaging in such analysis would cause the models to fall apart.

There is limited benefit in pointing out the differences between theological and economic methodology. We grant that theologians have properly called attention to certain anthropological and moral shortcomings in economics that we find to be intriguing. Our central question becomes: Do these insights move beyond the intriguing into the realm of the practical? Can we apply any of the personalist's theological insights to economics in order to reform the discipline of economics?

Possible Applications

Economists can utilize personalist thought by incorporating such concepts into their models. This would be more easily accomplished for theorists who already accept a methodologically subjective and methodologically individualistic framework. By recognizing the value that pertains to a given good or service results not from a quantifiable structure but an immeasurable and identifiable human propensity to act, economists are then able to incorporate a richer description of the human person. When they only focus on those characteristics that can be easily measured, the fullness of the human person is by necessity diminished. The human person is of secondary importance to the functioning of the model.

Subjective value theorists operate on the assumption that while it is impossible to understand the internal workings of the human mind, recognizing its role enables a fuller understanding of the human actions constituting economic activity. Value and action cannot rightly be created by fiat or by coercion. Personalists share many of the concerns that support methodological subjectivism and methodological individualism. They support free-market economists' concern for the negative effects on individuals of an activist central government, though for different reasons. Free-market economists are concerned due to the inefficiency that results when the government intervenes, while personalists are concerned due to the effect these actions have on the possibility of a fully human life. Since the goals of each do not contradict each other—in fact, they can be seen to enhance each other—both schools of thought can benefit by synthesizing the elements of their systems. Both would have an interest in criticizing the reductionism of the social sciences, maintaining the proper role of government, and focusing on the flourishing of the human person.

The area of human capital provides fertile soil for considering other possible applications. *Human capital*, a term associated with the work of Becker, has strong signification in both economics and theology. Personalists understand human capital in terms of the dignity of the human person and his or her inestimable worth. Economists understand human capital as a primary economic resource, which, when invested in, permits healthy returns in levels of productivity and development. Again, although the two disciplines speak differently about the same reality, the manner of their description is not contradictory but mutually enhancing.

Another possible area of research might be investigating elements of personalist thought in the history of economics. Many economists would easily fit within the personalists' camp. The Late Scholastic emphasis on natural law, the French recognition of the role of the entrepreneur in economic life, Carl Menger's explanation of subjective value theory, and Mises's introduction of praxeology all contain basic elements of personalist influence. Utilizing these traditions and others can bolster personalist thought. By attending to the economic aspects of the human person, personalists would be able to create an even fuller picture of the human person. Moreover, by attending to the human person as he or she is presented in social contexts, economists would be able to present a fuller picture of market activity.

Conclusion

It is not enough merely to identify similarities and differences between an economic approach and a theological one. Nor is it sufficient to highlight areas for constructive dialogue between personalists and free-market economists. What must be attempted is the actual insertion of personalist insight into economic modeling. Will such insights have any significant effect? The answer to this question, in large part, determines the ultimate usefulness and success of economic personalism as a new school of thought from the perspective of the economist. Therefore, our next chapter attempts such an integration.

Notes

1. We formulate this principle based on Becker's analysis of goods, which includes nonphysical goods and thus provides wider scope for human choice.

2. This situation applies to many disciplines that have economic implications but are not seriously considered by economists. Many theologians, for instance, write on economic matters but are typically ignored by economists. The *Journal of Markets and Morality* provides an interdisciplinary platform for both economists and theologians to communicate their insights.

3. Charles Issawi, *An Economic History of the Middle East and North Africa* (New York: Columbia University, 1982), 170-93.

4. Jude Wanniski, *The Way the World Works: How Economies Fail—and Succeed* (New York: Basic, 1978), 3-16.

5. Ludwig von Mises, *Human Action: A Treatise on Economics*, 3d rev. ed. (San Francisco: Fox and Wilkes, 1966), 32-34.

6. The effect of postmillennial eschatology on economic policy during the Progressive Era is discussed in Mark Thornton, *The Economics of Prohibition* (Salt Lake City: University of Utah Press, 1991).

4

Anthropology, Economics, and Culture

After our attempt at constructive dialogue between economics and personalism, why now raise the issue of culture? A dominant theme of the later half of the twentieth century has been the primacy of culture. Economic action does not take place in a vacuum. All social life takes place in and through culture. Therefore, the culture in which an economic system operates will influence how that economy operates. And the opposite is true—the culture will in turn be affected by the economic structures, and even the way economics as a discipline is construed.

There is a need for an economic personalism. This need can be seen more clearly when one examines the lack of a common cultural language for discussing the morality of market activity. Most attempts at moral analysis of economic phenomena tend to fall into a quasi-Marxist, left-wing ideological language and conceptual framework. Indeed, since the popularization of Marx and his ideas, those who support free-market economics have been on the defensive with respect to debates over economics and morality. The language, terminology, and approach of most modern individuals toward morality and markets are either to claim there is no connection or else to lapse into some version of Marxist social analysis.

We, therefore, have the odd situation of living in a world that practices global market economics of one variety or another, while retaining Marxist moral analyses of the same system. In other words, we lack a coherent, up-to-date defense of the moral superiority of economic liberty. There is no well-articulated personalist defense of the market. Our efforts attempt to remedy this situation. It is our belief that economic personalism has the potential to provide a common, coherent, analysis of our contemporary situation, thus eliminating the dichotomy between reality and our ability to analyze that reality morally.

Economic personalism can begin to provide the intellectual paradigm for revisioning our economic order. If we truly desire a humane economy—one that affirms the dignity of the human person and places the productive power of a free economic order at the service of that dignity—then we require a new moral paradigm for such analysis. Economic personalism's reliance on Christian social teaching, personalist anthropology, and free-market economics is such a paradigm.

The Meaning of Culture

Culture is a term often employed and seldom fully understood. It derives from the Latin word for *cultivation*—the turning over of soil—to make land fertile and ready to bear new life. To cultivate is to grow, to produce, to create new life. Sociologically speaking, culture refers to the way of life of a given people—their customs, habits, daily practices, values, and traditions. Food, style of clothing, dining habits, architecture, music, literature, and even sexual practices are reflective and formative of a people's culture. Culture—the totality of customs, traditions, and practices of a people—is a fundamental and pervasive phenomenon in every society. Beliefs, morals, and the customs of social relations are all influenced and, in part, shaped by culture. Culture provides the context for the meaning of life and the living of daily experiences.

Culture, unlike a political entity or structure, is engendered, not planned. Most matters of culture are engaged in unreflectively. Humans express and objectify themselves in and by culture. A person is, at the same time, subject and artisan of culture. Human cultures reflect the diversity of humanity itself. We cannot think of culture without thinking of human subjectivity and causality. Humankind is the primordial and fundamental fact of culture.[1] Culture is an expression of humankind. It is the confirmation of humanity. Humans create it, and by means of it, humanity creates itself. At the same time, we create culture in communion with others. Culture is a common expression of a people.[2] Culture is much like the air we breathe; we simply pay little attention to it on a daily basis, unless it is particularly sweet or bad. We live in and through our music, art, entertainment, conversation styles, and all other trappings of fashion and daily custom, as fish live in water. We flow through culture as culture flows from us. Culture flows from the soul of a people. Originating in the soul, culture reflects the state of the collective soul of a people. In both direct and indirect ways something as simple as how we greet one another is indicative of the condition of the soul of a people. Such claims require further clarification.

Consider something as simple as a greeting. Why do we greet people? We utter "hello" without even reflecting on what it means. It is routine, mundane, and yet significant. A gesture as simple as greeting a stranger in an elevator or passing on the street is full of meaning. Our greeting indicates the recognition of the other as person, or our desire to be polite, or our affirmation of our social nature, or our desire for community, or even merely our ability to form habits. All of these motivations are complicated, contain moral significance, and have spiritual overtones.

Ultimately, simple practices and acts in daily life—the things that express culture—reflect the state of our souls and our relationship with God. Consider the following: the person who uses foul language, dresses lewdly, and entertains other antisocial behaviors betrays the condition of his or her inner being. Although this is not an infallible method of analysis, most of us would judge the subjectivity of such a person to be lacking, not merely in social graces, but in more significant human traits. Of course, there always remain the uneducated, the newly emerging, and the social misfit who still possess a soul-openness and live their lives in accordance with the True, the Good, and the Beautiful. But, generally, the way one carries oneself through daily life speaks volumes about his or her inner condition.

Even in our age of the appreciation of other cultures (multiculturalism), we still esteem some cultures as worthy of praise and others of censure. We maintain a concern about the state of our culture, what it is doing to our youth, what it means for our future, and what it says about us as a people. Culture is a dynamic phenomenon, changing with the interior lives of the people who express it.

Historically, culture is cyclical and unpredictable. Tracing Western cultural history, we can identify the high points and low points of our civilization. These highs and lows correspond to a generation's way of life and how that generation faced God, moral values, and human dignity. Banal art, discordant music, sloppiness in daily life, shoddy workmanship, and antisocial manners indicate a people living less than their potential, out of touch with the finer aspects of their lives and the love of God. Such things go further than mere tackiness; they bespeak the poverty of one's soul.

Given the rapid pace of modern society, culture often changes within a generation. For older generations, the rigid structures of traditional culture are the necessary aspect of one's person and family life; they cannot be abandoned. The younger generations, on the other hand, often regard them as useless obstacles, and reject them to embrace new forms of social life. The communications revolution also presents a challenge to culture. More and more we are seeing the emergence of a unified world culture. This emerging uniformity of culture has both advantages and disadvantages. While it allows for easier communication and relations among diverse peoples, it also means the disappearance of ways of life that convey centuries of learned wisdom.

Regardless of changes, for culture to be in accord with human dignity and the value of human life, it must generate respect for basic human rights. Individual customs, practices, and traditions may differ and evolve, but respect for the basic human rights guarantees that cultures will affirm human dignity and respect the moral order. Any culture that respects and promotes such rights can be rightly said to be one worthy of humanity and Christianity.

Culture and Social Science

Social science studies human relationships and the institutions that arise from them. The social nature of the human person spills over into a complex web of interrelatedness throughout the social order. Repetition, necessity, tradition, all contribute to the development, often unplanned, of social structures such as the family, the corporation, the neighborhood, political organizations, and so on. These relationships and their resulting institutions form the core of society. Social science studies various social structures; economics examines the economy, political science analyzes the political institutions, and so on.

It would be mistaken to assume that the social scientist examines these realities from the perspective of cold, clear objectivity. The typical image of the social scientist is someone above the crowd, remotely observing the happenings around him or her, and taking extensive notes. Actually, the opposite is the case; social scientists operate from within the same structures they study. In a sense, it is impossible to escape culture, and therefore, the current culture provides the context for the study of anything within it. This fact allows for a dual insight: first, the culture of the social scientist will influence the actual practice of his or her discipline. Second, the practice of the discipline may in turn influence the culture. To further complicate the matter, various subcultures and cross-sections of the broader, common culture exist with varying degrees of affiliation. In a limited sense, it is proper to speak of the culture of the economics profession or the culture of any academic discipline. Therefore, we have three dynamics at work—the common culture, the subculture of the academic discipline, and the practice of the social science and its effects on both.

Social Science and the Common Culture

Pure objectivity in intellectual pursuits refers to, in one sense, the ability of the practitioner to transcend the limitations and horizons of his or her present historical–cultural circumstances. Every social scientist is necessarily a part of a given cultural context—a rich weave of the morals, values, traditions, dispositions, and daily habits of those around him or her. These peculiarities cannot but help have an effect on the practice of the discipline. The social scientist will import to his or her professional and scientific analysis, personal experience, values, and prejudices.

There has been much debate among philosophers of social science concerning these matters. On the one hand, the cultural context of the social scientist and the corresponding lack of objectivity are realities acknowledged, and even celebrated, by hermeneutical thinkers. The central contribution of hermeneutics to social science has been the understanding of the cultural bias of the social scientist. Knowing that such biases exist helps us better understand the actual usefulness and limitations of the disciplines themselves. Yet, most hermeneuticists revel in the lack of objectivity and celebrate its loss. They claim a certain methodological sophistication for having conceded to cultural reality.

Standing in opposition to the hermeneutical view of the social sciences is the more traditional Enlightenment approach to knowledge. Enlightenment thinkers and their heirs stress the necessity of the objectivity of the knower to guarantee the reliability of their findings. For these thinkers, cultural prejudices are considered to be obstacles to real knowledge, which requires objectivity. Friedrich von Hayek characterizes this attitude toward knowledge as objectivism. According to him,

> The attitude which, for want of a better term, we shall call the "objectivism" of the scientistic approach to the study of man and society, has found its most characteristic expression in the various attempts to dispense with our subjective knowledge of the working of the human mind, attempts which in various forms have affected almost all branches of social study. . . . A long series of thinkers have attempted to avoid the use of knowledge derived from "introspection."[3]

But, in Hayek's estimation, the bias against employing subjectively derived knowledge is doomed to failure, especially when it pertains to understanding human action. When an external stimulus that is thought to cause or occasion an action is defined in purely physical terms, then the observer has confined him- or herself to less than he or she can possibly know about the situation. Thus, Hayek argues,

> We know that people will react in the same way to external stimuli which according to all objective tests are different, and perhaps also that they will react in a completely different manner to a physically identical stimulus if it affects their bodies in different circumstances or at a different point. We know, in other words, that in his conscious decisions man classifies external stimuli in a way which we know solely from our own subjective experience of this kind of classification.[4]

From our perspective, both objectivism and hermeneutical thinking have merit within certain contexts. Social scientists ought to desire objectivity, but cultural determinates are indeed inescapable. How should this dilemma be resolved? Phenomenology has offered foundational insights for the construction of a balanced philosophy of social science.

The terms *phenomenology* and *hermeneutics* take into account wide and diverse philosophical schools of thought and are used to describe a wide range of philosophical approaches. A view common to all of them is that human perception occurs under cultural conditions that the subject brings to any experience. These conditions act as filters of experience—shaping our experience of the world.

Enlightenment thinkers have tended to view these cultural filters of perception as problematic. These influences on perception interfere with "true" understanding. Such filters create bias and are therefore thought of as obstacles to be overcome. Transcendence of these filters would be required to overcome the risk of subjectivism. Indeed, these cultural filters are akin to Kant's transcendental processes or structures of human consciousness. Kant's attempt at a transcendental critique of understanding led him to posit filters of human perception that altered our understanding of the world. Phenomenology arose in reaction to the placement of such limits on the transcendent quality of human knowledge.

According to phenomenology, true knowledge depends upon a sort of immaculate perception in which the subject is able to penetrate intellectually to the object itself (transcendence). This sort of epistemology presupposes a subject–object split. The presupposition is that in some sense you have reality in two parts: human subjects having perceptions of external and independent objects.[5] Gadamer, like many other hermeneutical thinkers, has rejected this subject–object dichotomy. Gadamer denies the possibility of this sort of perception:

> Perception conceived as an adequate response to a stimulus would never be a mere mirroring of what is there. For it would always remain an understanding of something as something. All understanding . . . is an articulation of what is there, in that it looks away from . . . looks at . . . sees together as. . . . There is no doubt that vision as an articulated reading of what is there removes, as it were, a lot of what is there from sight, so that for sight it is simply not there anymore. Equally it is led by its expectations to read in what is not there at all. Pure seeing and pure hearing are dogmatic abstractions which artificially reduce phenomena. Perception always includes meaning.[6]

For Gadamer, the subject's filters of perceptions are not obstacles to overcome but rather tools that can aid us in better understanding the world around us. Gadamer asserts that instead of attempting to transcend the subjective elements of experience we ought to learn from them, allowing them to help us understand what takes place in the act of knowing. Understanding is an experience in which both poles of experience contribute to the overall meaning. Meaning is therefore derived from the encounter as a whole and not from any one particular pole of the experience. Gadamer's understanding of hermeneutics has been influential in the philosophy of social science, economics in particular.

Phenomenology is a philosophical discipline whose aim is the clarification of the initial moments of perception. Phenomenology attempts to train the philosopher to overcome subjective obstacles in order to allow the object of perception to disclose itself clearly (*aletheia*). Phenomenology relies on an understanding of knowledge as receptive. The knower is receptive to the unfolding of the object. Phenomenology acknowledges that such understanding does not occur completely in a vacuum or outside of previous contexts, yet it allows for the transcendence of the possible distortions of subjectivity that may interfere with objectivity. Without phenomenology, hermeneutics seems doomed to an inescapable subjectivism due to its inability to ground a first moment of objective meaning based upon the receptive nature of human knowledge.

Our purpose is not to enter into the phenomenological–hermeneutical debate. Rather, our purpose in mentioning this debate is to highlight the interaction of culture and social science—both influence one another. If the question is raised concerning the effect of economics on the general culture, then a careful answer would require a multipart examination. The issue is not as simple as it first appears. We must continue our examination and consider the culture of the profession of economics itself.

The Subculture of Professional Economics

There is merit, albeit limited, in discussing the subculture of the economics profession. Taking economics as typical of most social sciences, we can continue our discussion of the relationship between culture and social science. There are established traditions, practices, even a particular language within modern economics. If we limit our scope to the American economics profession we find many common traits and cultural indicators. First, there is a relatively small number of individuals in the profession, with perhaps no more than twenty thousand economists in the United States. Second, many of them have been educated at a limited number of graduate educational facilities across the nation. These institutions share many traits in common, from their testing procedures, to requirements for qualifications, to content of curriculum. Receiving a higher degree in economics is really a passport into the language, customs, and habits of the professional economics guild.

The relatively small number of institutions and more or less uniform licensing procedures ensure that one can expect to find a high degree of uniformity throughout the profession. Most economists were given a similar education, encountered similar training, and approach problems in much the same manner.

Additionally, unlike other disciplines, the differences among economic schools of thought are not great. Unlike philosophy or theology, economics does not admit of hundreds of schools of thought varying greatly from one to another in terms of methodology and content. While there do exist varying schools of economic thought, the differences between them are slight.

Most mainstream economists share a common methodology, a tendency for mathematical modeling, and a bias toward positivistic formulations of their own discipline. Also shared are certain anthropological assumptions that can be roughly summarized in the model of homo economicus. While it is generally accepted that these reductionist features have practical value for the profession, such concepts cannot but help to influence the views of the individual economist who is immersed in them.

The Effects of Economics on the Common Culture

The specialized vocabularies of psychology, political science, and other social sciences, including economics, tend to become everyday terms and phrases. *Civil rights*, *income inequality*, *neurosis*—the list of terms that originated in social science research is lengthy. The mere existence of such a list is an indication that the social sciences, directly and indirectly, influence the common culture. While it may be true that the judgment of the social scientist is partially determined by his or her cultural context, the social scientist also shapes and alters the cultural context through the practice of his or her discipline. Imagine the differences in modern society if modern psychology had not become a recognized and reputable discipline. Similar statements hold for the discipline of economics.

Perhaps the central influence of economics on the common culture can be acknowledged in terms of how we view ourselves. One way in which the practice of social science affects the broader culture is by studiously avoiding the use of anthropological presuppositions. The human person is a creature constantly in search of meaning. In addition to searching for God, love, and questions of the origins of the cosmos, most people also search for the meaning of their own existence and questions of their identity. When the question, "Who am I?" is posed, answers are sometimes too readily adopted from the social sciences. Slowly, yet steadily, the image of the human person is recrafted into that of homo economicus.

The Culture of Homo Economicus

Homo economicus is the standard concept of the human person within economics. This understanding of the human person is a collection of presuppositions concerning the economic agent. The model of the human person that is now accepted by most mainstream economists is usually questioned by most philosophers and theologians. Questions arise concerning the model's accuracy and fullness, with frequent complaints that the current assumptions are reductionist and incomplete. Therefore, most philosophers and theologians—and nearly all personalists—would be critical of the economic vision of the human person. Yet, nearly all economic models at bottom maintain this vision of the human person. What is this vision? It consists of several components.

First, the person is viewed as an individual. The economist must first attempt to insert presuppositions based on *individual* human actions. Philosophically speaking, this is acceptable. There is no necessary denial of the social character of human nature. What we see in economics is methodological individualism—the focus on individual human actors to achieve scientific rigor.

Second, the individual human person is considered capable of action and choice. The economic concept of the human person is that of an acting person who chooses among various options. For many this element of exercising choice is also called freedom. Philosophically speaking, the economist's understanding of freedom usually fails to do justice to the richer theological and philosophical understandings of this faculty of the soul, yet it is not in direct contradiction with such theories either. There is, rather, a hint of reductionism. Human freedom is not considered in its fullness but rather reduced merely to the capacity for choice.

Third, the person is considered to be rational. Human action is thought to contain an inherent and discernible plan, a purpose, and a sense of order. The human person is operating from withimn a base of knowledge concerning economic activity and is choosing in accord with what he or she knows and values. Again, philosophically speaking, there is little problem with this presupposition.

Fourth, the person is considered to be self-interested. By this, the economist merely means to say that human beings act according to selected ends and their attainment. Self-interest is not posited as selfishness or a lack of concern for others and their needs. Rather, it is posited as an inherent and rational component of human action that people act to fulfill self-selected goals. Any theologian or philosopher can accept this presupposition, but only with qualifications concerning the exact definition of self-interest. Too narrow a definition of self-interest may border on selfishness and preclude any actions undertaken for the direct benefit of others.

Fifth, the person is considered to be motivated primarily by concerns of utility. Every human action is performed only after some cost-benefit analysis has been conducted. The chosen course of action is determined according to the value of utility. In fact, there is an implicit connection in the mind of many economists between rationality and the ability to perform successful cost-benefit analysis. Only action that corresponds to some recognizable utility function can be considered to be reasonable. Irrational behavior is that which has no underlying cost-benefit analysis. Of course, most philosophers would disagree with this depiction of both human reason and human motivation.

While the above traits of homo economicus are adequate for economic analysis, they must not be generalized. Economists build models on these anthropological assumptions, and the models prove useful for predictive economic analysis. Yet, philosophically speaking, these models are reductionist and lacking if they are presented as a full vision of human nature. They fail to present a completely accurate picture of the human person. Evidence of this inadequacy is seen once analysis is attempted concerning noneconomic goods such as love and family life.

A trend of the past fifteen years has been what might be termed *economic imperialism*.[7] Economic imperialism, sometimes also referred to as economism, indicates a radical economic interpretation of all spheres of human activity. In other words, all human behavior is analyzed in economic terms, through the filter of cost-benefit analysis. Two renowned economists associated with this unfortunate tendency are Richard Posner and Nobel prize winner Gary Becker.

Posner's book, *Sex and Reason*,[8] analyzes sexual behavior from a strictly economic model. The human actor is assumed to be homo economicus even for sexual decision making and behavior. Of course, it would be reasonable that some degree of utility maximization occurs in any human behavior and decision-making calculus, with sexual behavior being no exception. The mistake of Posner is that he, or more precisely those who take Posner's approach and absolutize it, falls prey to reductionism. Do arguments need to be advanced for the irrational aspects of sexual behavior? Clearly passion can inhibit a person's ability to make sound and reasonable judgments. The partner who enters into an extramarital affair does not always engage in a detailed cost-benefit analysis before cheating on his or her spouse. Actually, many who do commit infidelity later see the mistake of not conducting a prior cost-benefit analysis and thus regret their chosen course of action. Quite often the affair was not truly the result of an informed decision, but rather a choice made in the heat of the moment. Such a scenario illustrates, we think, the inability of rational-choice analysis to guide human decision making in all areas of human life. Where do concerns of love, fidelity, honor, and other such values—values that resist quantification and strict utility judgments—enter into Posner's rationalistic understanding of human sexual behavior? To sum up, we are not arguing that Posner's approach is completely invalid; in fact, his conclusions are insightful, useful, and make a genuine contribution to jurisprudence and social science methodology. Yet, from the perspective of economic personalism, we find that Posner's rational-choice analysis of human sexual behavior is reductionist and morally suspect.

Much of the same criticism advanced against Posner may also be applied to Gary Becker's analysis of marriage found in his recent work, *A Treatise on the Family.*[9] More than any other economist of our time, Becker has legitimized the application of neoclassical theory into areas previously considered taboo. Certainly other economists, many writing from the tradition of the Chicago School, previously examined areas such as crime, the family, and human capital; however, Becker brought these areas of study into the mainstream of microeconomic analysis. This is a significant accomplishment in a subject area in which most theorists are in fundamental agreement over major principles. For redefining this mainstream, Becker was certainly deserving of his Nobel prize in economics in 1992.

But while Becker's analysis of the family is the subject area for which he is most closely identified, it is also the area for which he is the most controversial. When Becker identifies the role of economic forces in the development and operation of families, he suggests reasons why the development of nontraditional, nonnuclear families is congruent with economic laws, and why their development is to be expected today and even predicted in the future. For instance, Becker recognizes that the primary motivating factor in human action is self-interest, an indisputable basis from which to begin. Most economists accept the self-interest axiom in the development of utility-maximizing models of human behavior. But Becker takes this axiom a step further and asserts that utility maximization applies to both market and nonmarket production. In this case, just as the individual who is not maximizing the profit received from market work is expected to search for ways to improve his or her return, even to the extent that he or she might switch jobs, so too is there a tendency to make the same corrections in nonmarket utility maximization. Since this production occurs primarily in the home, it explains why people tend to get married and also why people tend to get divorced. People will marry when they think that they can achieve a greater degree of utility in that state than when single, and they divorce when they feel that they can achieve a greater degree of utility in that state than when married. Thus, just as neoclassical theory explains why individuals change jobs, it explains changes in marital status as well.

Becker is certainly correct in identifying the primacy of economic laws in the ordering of the interpersonal relationships of both firms and families, but certainly the key to a happy and secure home life is somewhat more complex than the application of utility or profit-maximization analyses that normally apply to the study of economic behavior. Since his models possess predictive power, however, Becker's analysis can be extended to promote public provision of education or day-care services. For instance, because increases in human capital formation have resulted in increased incomes in the United States, state support for education is a self-justifying end. If single parents are hindered in the development of human capital, then state-financed day care can be (and is) similarly justified.

Yet, as with Posner's approach, economic personalists find key aspects of Becker's theory troubling as well. People that fall in love and marry are not, by and large, motivated principally by cost-benefit calculations. While there is certainly some degree of prior calculation that takes place before entering any significant relationship, it is inaccurate to characterize these relationships as resting on self-interested reasons alone. Consider the following set of options: Either people love others because they derive pleasure from doing so, or they love others because they determine the other to be worthy of such love. Which attitude captures the essence of genuine love? "I love you because you make me feel good," or "I love you because you are beautiful, good, and deserving of such a response"? One option has the motivation for love as self-satisfaction; the other option posits the meaning of love as the value of the beloved. Most people, it seems to us, prefer the second option and see its fuller, more humane character.

One goal of economic personalism is to free economics from the limitations of reductionism that threaten to translate into economism. Our concern with this form of disciplinary imperialism is not so much the analysis itself, but rather the cultural effects of the analysis. Through the work of other social scientists, members of the media, and educators in general,[10] there begins to be a slow acceptance that such forms of reductionism constitute the norm for understanding human behavior. Homo economicus, therefore, whether viewed from the perspective of rational-choice theory or economic imperialism, can serve economics well but can also damage culture in all too subtle ways.

Citing the poverty of homo economicus is interesting but inconsequential unless one points out the possible damage caused by such a viewpoint. The economics profession uses this model successfully to predict all sorts of human behaviors. Rather, the damage is cultural and occurs as the image of humans as rational self-maximizers eventually becomes accepted in mainstream society. Economists cannot be blamed for using or creating such models. The above assumptions are correct when confined to appropriate boundaries; they are simply not the only way to characterize human decision-making processes. Economics is a relatively successful discipline based on these presuppositions; however, our concern is with the cultural effect of these presuppositions.

One question at the heart of economic personalism concerns the lack of realism concerning how the economic concept of the person affects economics. Would greater anthropological realism result in greater predictive power? And second, how does such a view of the human person affect the broader culture? Could a fuller vision of the human person—one with enhanced presuppositions and controlled variables—permit greater predictive power and lead to enhanced economic modeling, thus improving the science of economics? We conclude that no answer is immediately apparent but that such an enterprise is worth undertaking. But what about the cultural effects of homo economicus? We believe that such a concept of the human person eventually trickles down into the mainstream culture. The economic view of human beings as rational self-maximizers can easily translate into a cultural understanding of human persons generally.

Individualism and Culture

A further concern with the concept of homo economicus is the possible misinterpretation of individualism that it promotes. The economist assumes an isolated individual for the sake of his or her study. The underlying and implicit vision is that of an entrepreneur, businessperson, or consumer acting according to an internal calculus and making decisions in isolation from others. The economist is merely attempting methodological simplicity through the application of methodological individualism. Few economists actually believe that humans are not socially natured or deny the communal aspect of human existence.

Yet it is too often the case that methodological individualism is either taken to mean or imply moral individualism. Moral individualism entails living life completely for one's own sake, blind to the needs of others, and failing to maintain lasting social relationships. Such individualism is contrary to human nature and the common good. Stirred by greed and motivated only by self-interest, individuals can place themselves over one another as they struggle for sustenance and desired goods and services. Thus, they become isolated and detached as a result of focusing exclusively on their own needs and interests to the exclusion of anyone else's needs. Society suffers as community breaks down and people treat one another with suspicion.

The tendency in anthropology is to conceive of the human situation as the individual versus the community, or to create a tension between the rights of individuals. The recognition that the human person is the fundamental building block for society in no way requires us to deny the social nature of the person or the importance of community. The person is prior to the group as people are prior to the state. Part of what it means to be a flourishing human person is to be in relationship with others. Persons are born in and for community. Our being is that of relation—we are always someone's son or daughter, mother or father, brother or sister, even neighbor and friend. Our concern is with the relationship between the subjectivity of the person as an individual and the structure of the human community.

A community does not take shape merely because several people live and act together or because one person interacts with others. Community does not simply denote an aggregate of individuals, but a unity of persons in a common culture. In this respect, culture is prior to community. But any investigation of a given aggregate cannot simply posit an objective reality that affects every member of a social unit equally; rather it must make a point of focusing on the consciousness and personal experience of the members—as it were—individually. Only by taking this approach do we perceive the reality of a community and begin to grasp its essential meaning.[11] A proper understanding of the role of the individual in social science augments and helps to prevent interpretations of moral individualism.

Consumerism and Culture

The professional economist, acting as an economist, conceives of people primarily as consumers. Individuals are seen in terms of their capacity to utilize resources and wealth. This vision of the person does not preclude his or her ability to produce goods, yet most modeling favors the image of consumption over that of production. The perception of the human person as a consumer can lead to the phenomenon of consumerism.

Consumerism is a complex phenomenon that must be carefully defined. If we are to understand this genuine threat to culture we must be perfectly clear about its origins, parameters, and essential characteristics. Consumerism is usually taken to be a culture's obsession with shopping and buying. The result is that people begin to view their value as persons in relation to their possessions and consumption patterns. Usually, such a situation is blamed on the market economy. Yet, if examined carefully, consumerism is really a malfunction of the human heart. It is the idolatry of wealth. A consumerist mindset is one in which possessions become the central expressions of identity, values, and love.

> Consumerism is, quite precisely, the consuming of life by the things consumed. It is living in a manner that is measured by having rather than being. As John Paul makes clear, consumerism is hardly the sin of the rich. The poor, driven by discontent and envy, may be consumed by what they do not have as the rich are consumed by what they do have. The question is not, certainly not most importantly, a question about economics. It is first and foremost a cultural and moral problem requiring a cultural and moral remedy.[12]

Affluence brought about by markets and human labor can influence the moral climate of a culture. Living in conditions where essential goods and services are abundant does produce a different mindset. However, it must be noted that the poor in primitive societies fall prey to similar defects. Envy, greed, and unhealthy attitudes toward wealth are not dependent upon the amount of wealth present within a society. People will envy and worship mud huts as quickly as they will seaside mansions. Although the increased presence of wealth changes the situation slightly, the actual amount of wealth and its immediate character are not the core issues in consumerism.

The person who understands the creation and proper use of wealth as a God-given calling can maintain the correct ordering of his soul: He or she will not confuse *having* with *being* because they know that in the face of responsibilities from an eternal God, transitory material wealth can never substitute for the fact that "in Him we live, move, and have our being." The person who understands his or her life's work as a vocation will see the world through the eyes of the eternal; not to deny the importance of material goods, of course, but rather to keep their eternal significance in proper perspective.

Conclusion

The tenor of this chapter has been critical of some of the more subtle effects of professional economics on mainstream culture and morals. The reductionist tendencies of the economics profession—albeit necessary—are troubling to theologians and moral philosophers and, they believe, pose hazards to the general culture. However, it is essential that the positive contribution of economics to culture and human welfare be recognized.

An implicit theme of this volume, and, in fact, of the project of economic personalism in general, has been the mutual benefit of dialogue between economists and theologians. Nevertheless, we would be remiss if we did not acknowledge that most theologians underestimate and undervalue the contributions of economics as a profession and a social science. The ongoing revolution of the global economic market is a testament to the convincing efforts and sound analysis of economists who understood key aspects of human behavior and the inner logic of choice. The continuing improvement in world nutrition, standards of living, and genuine human welfare must, in part, be attributed to the rhetorical and intellectual contributions of those economists who have supported free-market reforms and advised governments and policymakers about the advantages of economic liberty.

Social scientists such as Milton Friedman, Friedrich von Hayek, and other economists have been effective defenders of human liberty and improved human standards of living. Even the work of Gary Becker, though criticized above, cannot and should not be summarily dismissed. Becker's work in the areas of human capital and the economics of the family, in addition to his service on the Pontifical Council of Social Science, demonstrates his good intentions and the benefit of his contributions—the reductionism not withstanding. Therefore, let us not conclude this chapter without honoring the insights and efforts of economists and the value of economics for the promotion of human welfare. The goal of this work has been to engage economists and theologians in constructive dialogue with the aim of generating a more humane, accurate, and dignity-affirming social science.

Notes

1. John Paul II, "Address to UNESCO," Paris, June 1980.
2. John Paul II, "Address in Gniezno," Poland, June 1979.
3. Friedrich von Hayek, *The Counter-Revolution of Science: Studies on the Abuse of Reason* (Indianapolis: Liberty Press, 1979), 78.
4. Hayek, *Counter-Revolution of Science*, 43.
5. This is not to deny that some objects are ideal as opposed to real, and that some objects are not external but internal to the consciousness of the subject.
6. Hans-Georg Gadamer, *Truth and Method* (London: Sheed and Ward, 1979), 81.
7. Cf. Jesús M. Zaratiegui, "The Imperialism of Economics over Ethics," *Journal of Markets and Morality* 2, no. 2 (Fall 1999): 208-19.
8. Richard A. Posner, *Sex and Reason* (Cambridge, Mass.: Harvard University Press, 1992).
9. Gary S. Becker, *A Treatise on the Family* (Cambridge, Mass.: Harvard University Press, 1991).
10. Cf. Anthony M. Yezer, Robert S. Goldfarb, and Paul J. Poppen, "Does Studying Economics Discourage Cooperation? Watch What We Do, Not What We Say or How We Play," *Journal of Economic Perspectives* 10, no. 1 (1996): 178; and Robert H. Frank, Thomas D. Gilovich, and Denise T. Regan, "Does Studying Economics Inhibit Cooperation?" *Journal of Economic Perspectives* 7, no. 2 (1993): 159.
11. Karol Wojtyla, "The Controversy about Man," in *Toward a Philosophy of Praxis: An Anthology*, ed. Alfred Bloch and George T. Czuczka (New York: Crossroad, 1981), 25.
12. Richard John Neuhaus, *Doing Well and Doing Good: The Challenge to the Christian Capitalist* (New York: Doubleday, 1992), 52-53.

CONCLUSION

This work was intended to be a dialogue between economists and theologians on the subject of anthropology. The concept of the human person inherent, implicitly or explicitly, in any academic discipline significantly affects the outcomes, methodologies, and even the self-understanding of the discipline. For our purposes, however, the conversation has involved the contributions of theologians and economists to arrive at a synthesis that might fall under the rubric of economic personalism. Our conversation has yielded the result of improved mutual understanding and has deepened our knowledge of the anthropology of both personalism and economics. It will be useful to recapitulate here the main themes of the project to offer a concise and coherent statement of just what has been accomplished.

We began by explicating the principal tenets of a theological anthropology. This is the personalism side of the equation, the theological and philosophical approach to reality that takes as its most basic point of reference the human person. Every human person, we argued, is a reflection of the imago Dei—he or she is created in the image of God. Simply stated, to be created in the image of God is to be made a person—a rational, emotive, and volitional being. Such qualities and the implied relationship with the Divine bespeaks the immense value of the person. This recognition requires that every person be treated with a dignity befitting such lofty origins.

Yet, even beyond the anthropological insights spoken of above, personalist thought continues to inform our discussion. Further insights from personalist authors note that every human being is a moral agent, capable of action that fulfills or undermines the imago Dei. The person as a moral agent implies several dimensions, including the possession of reason and will, the possession of a communal and social nature, and the capacity for relationship with God. Finally, moral ability implies the existence of sin, and the reality that sin has a corrupting influence on both human nature and human action.

Christian personalism, we believe, most accurately incorporates these basic presuppositions and reflects on them in a way that lends itself to useful dialogue with the discipline of economics. Karol Wojtyla is the key figure here, the Polish personalist who synthesized the work of French and German personalist and phenomenological thinkers with orthodox Christian theology.

The other side of the equation is economics. We surveyed the historical development of economics as a discipline, noting how its positivist tendency came to dominate the profession during the twentieth century. At the same time, however, there remained among some economists a philosophical outlook that could lend itself more readily to dialogue with Christian personalism. We note here at the conclusion that the development of economics as a positive discipline is not completely tragic, but that it is only the reductionist tendencies of positivism about which theologians and ethicists express concern.

The contemporary formulation of the positivist trajectory in economics can be seen in adherents of the Virginia and Chicago Schools. Practitioners in these schools employ strictly empirical methods, and mathematics plays an indispensable role in their economic analysis. While we concede a certain utility to these approaches, nevertheless, we believe that of all the free-market schools, the Austrian School is, perhaps, the most conducive for the type of synthesis we attempt. Austrian economists, while being far from mainstream and confounded at times by methodological issues, provide a suitable dialogue partner for our purpose. Ultimately, it is our intent to expand the dialogue of economic personalism beyond that of the Austrian School to all standard neoclassical and nonmainstream economists. Austrian School conclusions are not really at odds with other neoclassical approaches to economics, particularly with respect to the role of the state. Yet, Austrian economists have always maintained a more philosophical, deductive method that serves to make points of contact with personalism more apparent.

Economists, whether Austrian or not, rely on models of human behavior for predictive and descriptive work. Underlying these models of human behavior reside ideas and assumptions about human motivation, value, and decision making. Essentially, these assumptions, when taken as a whole, form an implicit anthropology. This anthropological model is often referred to as homo economicus. The distinguishing characteristic of homo economicus is rational choice motivated by utility maximization understood as enlightened self-interest. While theologians may resist such a conceptualization of the human person, they must also realize that such a description, while being incomplete, is also fairly accurate and highly useful to the social scientist.

Part of the process of synthesizing economics and moral theology involves critically engaging the social science paradigm of homo economicus. We thus undertook an analysis of economic methods from the perspective of the moral theologian. However, we affirmed at the outset that theologians have little to say regarding the usefulness of economics. That is, it must be conceded that economic models work in that they serve well the purposes of their practitioners. Nevertheless, this admission does not preclude the possibility that theologians may contribute some important observations about economics as a discipline, particularly with respect to taking the human person as the primary point of contact between the fields of study. Furthermore, the contributors to this volume are encouraged by the prospect that future generations of social scientists, relying on the more accurate theological insights of personalist anthropology, might actually improve the predictive and descriptive power of economics.

To this end, therefore, the theologian voices five areas of concern. The first follows from the premise of the centrality of the human person. Economists should take steps to acknowledge that the acting person is the most important unit of economic analysis. Thus, excessive focus placed on impersonal phenomena such as money supply or business cycles might work as cross-purposes to this recognition. While economic indicators are certainly essential to the economist's task, it is often the case that preoccupation with such phenomena leads to a depersonalization of the economy, thus viewing the market in essentially mechanistic terms.

The second concern is the danger inherent in presupposing methodological individualism. Many theologians appreciate the value of this approach for economic analysis, but warn against the tendency for individualism to spill over into moral and social theory and therefore deny the social nature of the human person. The concern here is not with focusing on the concrete human individual, for theologians readily admit to the ontological priority of the concrete human person; rather it is with the possible moral individualism that can creep into social science analysis. This creeping moral individualism may lead to an atomistic view of society and the diminishment, if not denial, of human social nature.

Furthermore, moral theologians characteristically encourage economists to acknowledge that the demands of justice and charity must enter into every sphere of human existence. Market analysis that ignores such concerns fails to consider the human person in his or her fullness. Fortunately, most economists understand that the faithful practice of their discipline contributes to human betterment only if it actually leads to economic development.

The fourth concern the moral theologian offers the economist is the fact that understanding persons as homo economicus does not exhaust their meaning. The central complaint of the theologian has to do with the tendency toward reductionism in social science. There are phenomena of human life that transcend economic analysis to which harm is done when economists engage in "economic imperialism" and seek to explain these phenomena solely in utilitarian terms. Marriage and family are good examples of such phenomena. There are aspects of human life, values, and human goods that preclude analysis from the perspective of utility.

Finally, theologians caution that economists must also be careful not to ignore the importance of nonmarket, nonproductive facets of human society in their analysis of human behavior. In their zeal to subject human interaction to economic analysis, economists sometimes exhibit the tendency to pass over groups such as children, stay-at-home parents, and the handicapped—that is, anyone who does not figure in the normal scheme of production and consumption. The economy is a complex web of human relationships—buying, selling, trading, and so on—most of these activities happen, not in the board rooms of major corporations, but in the homes of the smaller towns that populate the landscape of the Western world.

Moral theologians are not the only partners in this dialogue to offer criticism and commentary. How do economists view the potential of a synthesis in the form of economic personalism? Admittedly, for them, there are certain difficulties to overcome, but personalist theology also maintains certain advantages that other forms of religious thinking do not.

It is difficult, as economists observe, for contemporary professional economists to engage in personalist reflection because of the incentive structure of the profession, which makes innovation risky. At the same time, the history of economics shows that those systems that focus on the individual actor as opposed to impersonal forces generally enjoy more long-term success and public credibility. In addition, many early personalists, while not concerned with economic freedom, per se, were sensitive to the pernicious effects of expansive state power. These two facts provide historical precedent for the plausibility of the synthesis being proposed throughout this book.

One particularly difficult obstacle that personalism encounters in neoclassical economics is the latter's obsessive concern with predictive accuracy. If all that economists are concerned about is the predictive power of their models, then personalism cannot offer much in the way of criticism or benefit. On this point, the Austrian approach once again lends itself especially to our project, because of its ability to entertain the multifaceted nature of the human being and its modesty with respect to economic forecasting.

Economists raise the practical, but not unimportant issue, that they are trained as social scientists, not as theologians or philosophers. The lack of appreciation for economics among some moral theologians has its own version within the economics profession. Many economists merely want to work with models and conduct analysis with little or no regard for the larger questions that their methodology raises. They are not overly concerned with normative questions of methodology, the ontological status of the human person, or which system of moral analysis enjoys favor in theological circles. Furthermore, most economists, though practicing a reductionism in their professional work, do not personally believe or subscribe to this conceptual picture of the human person. The average economist does not raise his or her children according to strict cost-benefit analysis. Attempts must always be made to demonstrate the utility of the proposed synthesis in order to entice economists to grapple with more philosophical approaches and questions.

This book has offered at least two points on which economic personalism can be said to have found the possibility for fruitful dialogue. The first is the topic of subjective value theory. Personalist theology finds much to applaud in the view, from an economic perspective, that human choices determine the value of an economic good, rather than an objective quantifiable calculation. This view places the person and human liberty at the center of the economic system, and consigns material objects to a secondary role.

Another intriguing point of contact is found in the notion of human capital. At first glance the term *capital* may not seem to function as a personalist appellation, but the idea behind the term is consonant with personalist anthropology. For the economist employing the idea of human capital, the human being is a fundamentally positive entity. The person is a resource—creative and productive—not a drain on society or one animal among many vying for a limited pool of goods. For the personalist, the notion of human capital is one that upholds human dignity, a hopeful sign of potential interchange between economics and theology.

The ideas of value subjectivity and human capital are economic insights that might aid personalists in their philosophical reflections on the person. The goal of economic personalism is that by attending to the economic aspects of the person, personalists might be able to arrive at a fuller picture of the human person. Thus, for economists, by attending to the human person in his or her social context, they may be able to present a fuller picture of market activity.

In terms of its wider cultural and intellectual significance, it is hoped that economic personalism will provide a new paradigm for understanding the moral dimensions of the free economy. While it is true that free-market systems have almost universally been vindicated on the world scene (vis-à-vis their socialist counterparts), there has been no systematic attempt to analyze the market economic structure in moral terms. When such discussion does occur, however, a criticism of the free market in Marxist language and categories is usually the result. Economic personalism aims to provide a moral context for the free market without recourse to Marxist moralizing.

Through these means, therefore, economic personalism desires to challenge the cultural effects of the reigning view of human beings as homo economicus. The typical economic view of the person as an individual, capable of free action, who is rational, self-interested, and utility maximizing is, for reasons we have already explored, deficient. This criticism is not intended to undermine the efficacy of economics; rather, we believe that an economics that takes into account the fuller picture of the person may in fact render the profession more effective, more predictive, and more realistic. Reforming economics in this way may be the first step toward repairing the cultural damage done by the society-wide embrace of homo economicus. Radical moral individualism and consumerism are two serious problems plaguing many free-market nations, and economic personalism may be a key part of preserving the fundamentally sound economic arrangement of the free market while simultaneously ameliorating the cultural degradation threatening the spiritual health of persons who act in such arenas.

BIBLIOGRAPHY

Augustine. "On Original Sin." In *Augustine of Hippo: Selected Writings*. Edited and translated by Mary T. Clark. New York: Paulist Press, 1984.

Becker, Gary S. *Human Capital: A Theoretical and Empirical Analysis, with Special Reference to Education*. New York: National Bureau of Economic Research, 1966.

______. *A Treatise on the Family*. Cambridge, Mass.: Harvard University Press, 1991.

Bell, John F. *A History of Economic Thought*. New York: Ronald Press, 1967.

Blaug, Mark. *Great Economists since Keynes: An Introduction to the Lives and Works of One Hundred Modern Economists*. Totowa, N.J.: Barnes and Noble, 1985.

Böckle, Franz, ed. *Moral Problems and Christian Personalism*. Mahweh, N.J.: Paulist Press, 1965.

Brunner, Emil. *Dogmatics*. Vol. 2. *The Christian Doctrine of Creation and Redemption*. Translated by Olive Wyon. Philadelphia: Westminster Press, 1952.

______. *Man in Revolt: A Christian Anthropology*. Translated by Olive Wyon. New York: Charles Scribner's Sons, 1939.

______. *The Christian Understanding of Man*. London: Willett, Clark & Co., 1938.

Burns, J. Patout, ed. *Theological Anthropology*. Philadelphia: Fortress Press, 1981.

Chafuen, Alejandro A. *Christians for Freedom: Late-Scholastic Economics*. San Francisco: Ignatius Press, 1986.

Cochran, John P., and Fred R. Glahe. *The Hayek–Keynes Debate: Lessons for Current Business Cycle Research*. Lewiston, N.Y.: Edwin Mellon Press, 1999.

Danielou, Jean. *Gospel Message and Hellenistic Culture*. Edited and translated by John Austin Baker. Philadelphia: Westminster Press, 1973.

de Lubac, Henri. *Catholicism: Christ and the Common Destiny of Man*. Translated by Lancelot C. Sheppard and Elizabeth Englund. San Francisco: Ignatius Press, 1988.

______. *The Drama of Atheist Humanism*. Translated by Edith M. Riley. Cleveland: World Publishing, 1963.

Ekelund, Robert B., Jr., and Robert F. Hebert. *A History of Economic Theory and Method*. New York: McGraw-Hill, 1975.

Ford, David F. *The Modern Theologians: An Introduction to Christian Theology in the Twentieth Century*. 2d ed. Cambridge, Mass.: Blackwell, 1997.

Frank, Robert H., Thomas D. Gilovich, and Denise T. Regan. "Does Studying Economics Inhibit Cooperation?" *Journal of Economic Perspectives* 7, no. 2 (1993): 154-67.

Friedman, Milton. *Capitalism and Freedom*. With the Assistance of Rose D. Friedman. Chicago: University of Chicago Press, 1962.

______. *Dollars and Deficits: Living with America's Economic Problems*. Englewood, N.J.: Prentice-Hall, 1968.

______. *Price Theory: A Provisional Text*. Rev. ed. Chicago: Aldine, 1970.

Gadamer, Hans-Georg. *Truth and Method*. London: Sheed and Ward, 1979.

Guardini, Romano. *Person and World*. Translated by Stella Lange. Chicago: Regnery, 1965.

Holcombe, Randall G. *Economic Models and Methodology*. New York: Greenwood, 1989.

Hughes, Philip Edgcumbe. *Creative Minds in Contemporary Theology: A Guidebook to the Principal Teachings of Karl Barth, G. C. Berkouwer, Emil Brunner, Rudolf Bultmann, Oscar Cullmann, James Denney, C. H. Dodd, Herman Dooyeweerd, P. T. Forsyth, Charles Gore, Reinhold Niebuhr, Pierre Teilhard de Chardin, and Paul Tillich*. Grand Rapids, Mich.: Wm. B. Eerdmans, 1966.

Issawi, Charles. *An Economic History of the Middle East and North Africa*. New York: Columbia University, 1982.

John Paul II. "Address in Gniezno." Poland, June 1979.

______. "Address to UNESCO." Paris, June 1980.

______. "Analysis of the Biblical Account of Creation." In *The Theology of the Body: Human Love in the Divine Plan*. Boston: Pauline Books and Media, 1997.

Also see Wojtyla, Karol.

Lauer, Eugene, and Joel Mecko, eds. *A Christian Understanding of the Human Person: Basic Readings*. New York: Paulist Press, 1982.

Maritain, Jacques. *Freedom in the Modern World*. Translated by Richard O'Sullivan. New York: Gordian Press, 1971.

Marshall, Alfred. *Principles of Economics: An Introductory Volume*. 8th ed. London: Macmillan, 1920.

Meek, Roland L. *The Economics of Physiocracy: Essays and Translations*. London: George Allen & Unwin, 1962.

Molina, Luis de. *La Teoria del Justo Precio*. Madrid: Ed. Nacional, 1981.

Mounier, Emmanuel. *Personalism*. Translated by Philip Mairet. Notre Dame: University of Notre Dame Press, 1952.

Neuhaus, Richard John. *Doing Well and Doing Good: The Challenge to the Christian Capitalist*. New York: Doubleday, 1992.

Niebuhr, Reinhold. *The Nature and Destiny of Man*. Vols. 1 and 2. New York: Charles Scribner's Sons, 1949.

Pannenberg, Wolfhart. *Anthropology in Theological Perspective*. Translated by Matthew J. O'Connell. Philadelphia: Westminster Press, 1985.

Pelikan, Jaroslav. *The Emergence of the Catholic Tradition (100-600)*. Vol. 1. Chicago: University of Chicago Press, 1971.

Posner, Richard A. *Sex and Reason*. Cambridge, Mass.: Harvard University Press, 1992.

Rahner, Karl. *Grace in Freedom*. Translated by Hilda Graef. New York: Herder and Herder, 1969.

Ratzinger, J. Foreword to Henri de Lubac, *Catholicism: Christ and the Common Destiny of Man*. Translated by Lancelot C. Sheppard and Elizabeth Englund. San Francisco: Ignatius Press, 1988.

Rauch, Rufus William, Jr. Foreword to Emmanuel Mounier, *Personalism*. Translated by Philip Mairet. Notre Dame: University of Notre Dame Press, 1952.

Rothbard, Murray N. *Economic Thought before Adam Smith: An Austrian Perspective on the History of Economic Thought*. Vol. 1. Hanks, U.K.: Edward Elgar, 1995.

______. "New Light on the Prehistory of Austrian Economics." In *The Foundations of Modern Austrian Economics*. Edited by E. G. Dolan. Mission, Kans.: Sheed and Ward, 1976.

Samuelson, Paul A. *Foundations of Economic Analysis*. Cambridge, Mass.: Harvard University Press, 1947.

Saravia, Luis de la Calle. "Instruccion de Mercadres (1544)." In *The School of Salamanca: Readings in Spanish Monetary Theory, 1544-1605*. Edited and translated by Marjorie Grice-Hutchinson. Oxford, U.K.: Clarendon Press, 1952.

Scheler, Max. *Formalism in Ethics and Non-Formal Ethics of Values: A New Attempt Toward the Foundation of an Ethical Personalism*. Translated by Manfred S. Frings and Roger L. Funk. Evanston, Ill.: Northwestern University Press, 1973.

______. *On the Eternal in Man*. Translated by Bernard Noble. London: SCM Press, 1960.

Schumpeter, Joseph A. *History of Economic Analysis*. New York: Oxford University Press, 1954.

Scola, Angelo. *Hans Urs von Balthasar: A Theological Style*. Grand Rapids, Mich.: Wm. B. Eerdmans, 1995.

Stigler, George. *The Citizen and the State: Essays on Regulation*. Chicago: University of Chicago Press, 1975.

Thornton, Mark. *The Economics of Prohibition*. Salt Lake City: University of Utah Press, 1991.

von Balthasar, Hans Urs. *The Glory of the Lord: A Theological Aesthetics*. Translated by Erasmo Leiva-Merikakis. Edited by Joseph Fessio, S. J., and John Riches. San Francisco: Ignatius Press; New York: Crossroad, 1961-1969.

von Hayek, Friedrich. *The Counter-Revolution of Science: Studies on the Abuse of Reason*. Indianapolis: Liberty Press, 1979.

______. "The Use of Knowledge in Society." In *The Essence of Hayek*. Edited by Chiaki Nishiyama and Kurt R. Leube. Stanford, Calif.: Hoover Institution Press, 1984.

von Mises, Ludwig. *Human Action: A Treatise on Economics*. 3d rev. ed. San Francisco: Fox and Wilkes, 1966.

Wanniski, Jude. *The Way the World Works: How Economies Fail—and Succeed*. New York: Basic, 1978.

Williams, George Huntston. *The Mind of John Paul II: Origins of His Thought and Action*. New York: Seabury Press, 1981.

Wojtyla, Karol. *The Acting Person*. Translated by A. Potocki. Dordrecht, Netherlands: D. Reidel, 1979.

______. *Toward a Philosophy of Praxis: An Anthology*. Edited by Alfred Bloch and George T. Czuczka. New York: Crossroad, 1981.

Yezer, Anthony M., Robert S. Goldfarb, and Paul J. Poppen. "Does Studying Economics Discourage Cooperation? Watch What We Do, Not What We Say or How We Play." *Journal of Economic Perspectives* 10, no. 1 (1996): 170-84.

Zaratiegui, Jesús M. "The Imperialism of Economics over Ethics." *Journal of Markets and Morality* 2, no. 2 (Fall 1999): 208-19.

INDEX

ABOUT THE AUTHORS

Patricia Donohue-White (S.T.L., Lateran University, Rome) currently teaches theology at Franciscan University of Steubenville in Ohio. She earned her B.A. in philosophy and theology from Magdalen College in New Hampshire and is currently completing her Ph.D. in philosophy at the International Academy of Philosophy in Schaan, Liechtenstein. Her research interests include Christian feminism, the personalism of John Paul II, and the theology of marriage and family.

Stephen J. Grabill is research fellow and executive editor of the *Journal of Markets and Morality* at the Center for Economic Personalism. He is currently completing his Ph.D. in systematic theology from Calvin Theological Seminary, where he also received his Th.M. and M.T.S. degrees. He earned his B.A. degrees in philosophy and political science from Liberty University in Lynchburg, Virginia. His areas of specialization include reformed social ethics, natural-law theory, theological methodology, theology and the philosophy of science, and the thought of Abraham Kuyper and Wolfhart Pannenberg.

Christopher Westley (Ph.D., Auburn University) is an assistant professor of economics at Jacksonville State University. His research interests include public choice theory, Austrian economics, and the history of economic thought.

Gloria Zúñiga (Ph.D., University at Buffalo) is a research fellow at the Center for Economic Personalism. She recently completed her dissertation titled *A General Theory of Value: Axiology in the Central European Philosophical Tradition*. Her areas of specialization include value theory, moral philosophy, and the philosophy of economics.

ABOUT THE CENTER FOR ECONOMIC PERSONALISM

The **Center for Economic Personalism** (CEP) is a subsidiary research facility within the Acton Institute for the Study of Religion and Liberty. The CEP seeks to integrate free-market economic theory with Christian social thought to advance a humane economy. It does this by producing scholarly books, monographs, and a refereed academic publication, the *Journal of Markets and Morality*. The CEP also provides academic advising, research assistance, and bibliographical materials.

The **Acton Institute for the Study of Religion and Liberty** is a nonprofit, educational organization that seeks to promote a free and virtuous society characterized by individual liberty and sustained by religious principles. The Institute seeks to inform religious and business leaders on the moral dimensions of the free economy through conferences, lectures, and publications.

Center for Economic Personalism
Acton Institute for the Study of Religion and Liberty
161 Ottawa, Northwest, Suite 301
Grand Rapids, Michigan 49503

Phone: (616) 454-3080 • Fax: (616) 454-9454
E-mail: cep@acton.org
http://www.acton.org/cep

www.ingramcontent.com/pod-product-compliance
Ingram Content Group UK Ltd.
Pitfield, Milton Keynes, MK11 3LW, UK
UKHW021034150926
475561UK00003B/96